FEEL. LOVE. NOW...

Creating Stability and Wellness
in the Whirlwinds of Change

EREZ ASCHER

SOTERIAN
PUBLISHING

SANTA BARBARA, CA

Author: Erez Ascher
Cover Design & Illustrations: Juraj Sedlák
Body Design: Jennifer Thomas, Beyond Words Editing

ISBN: 978-1-949682-02-1 (Paperback)
ISBN: 978-1-949682-03-8 (eBook)
LCCN: 2021905877
First Edition 2021
Published in the United States of America

Dedicated to
the memory of
Anne Leslie Hawkins (Lambert)

Contents

Contents

Contents

Introduction

Ever more rapidly, our world is changing – and we are changing with it. Within ourselves, in our relationships, in our communities, and in our societies, we are experiencing different forms of growth. Yet inevitably, our growth comes with growing pains – which at times can be quite intense.

The confusion and disorientation of rapid change can feel like being caught in a hurricane. You may feel urges within yourself to hide, to distract yourself, to sleep it off, or to hope that it will just go away. But, life doesn't work that way.

As living beings, we grow even as we deteriorate. We change – and our world changes as well. It, too, is alive. It, too, is growing – even when it, too, deteriorates. Creating a life of wellness, happiness, and stability in such a rapidly changing world can feel difficult, overwhelming, and even impossible.

The tools and guidelines that worked well in a world that was *slow* to change are no longer reliable and sometimes even harmful to use. When our old maps of life are no longer accurate, it's easy to become lost. And, in a rapidly shifting world, it's simply *not possible* for you to find or create an unchanging map to show you which path is best for you to take. But, you *can* create a real-time navigation system for your life – and *Feel. Love. Now...* was created to show you how to do just that.

WHAT LED TO IT?

It was the summer of 2012 when I discovered that I was lost – very lost, in fact. Having a beautiful house, a beautiful wife, a flexible job, and a rather beautiful life were supposed to be resulting in my happiness, I thought. Instead, all I seemed to be feeling was misery. But, how was that even possible?

I had done what I was "supposed to do". I had been "the good student". I had been "the valuable resource". I even had a good credit score. But, none of that mattered to my heart. None of that mattered to my soul. It seemed that being "good" and "valued" had nothing to do with my happiness. In fact, I was a wreck, stuck on a sandbank in what were clearly marked as open waters on my map of life.

Thus began my midlife crisis – and my spiritual awakening. I let go – of my beautiful marriage and my beautiful house, my flexible job and my rather beautiful life. I realized how lost I was. So, I began to explore my surroundings. Surely there must be a path, a path that would lead me somewhere better than where I was. Surely one of those paths would lead me to a place of happiness and fulfillment – somewhere and somehow.

For years, I searched for the "right" path – and for years I kept finding paths that led me off in new directions. I was learning, still being "the good student". But, this time, I was being a good student of life. I discovered things *far* beyond what I had previously imagined possible. And, in the process, I discovered that the world was changing more *drastically* than I'd thought possible. It turned out that the paths I'd hoped would lead me to happiness and fulfillment were now leading to very different destinations than the ones I'd intended!

It no longer made sense for me to look for a well-worn trail to take me to where I wanted to be. What I needed was a *guidance system* to show me the most useful way to proceed, in order for me to make *my own* path in each moment – guiding me to my chosen destinations.

So, I began to build – and to test, adjusting and improving it to make it more accurate over time. For years, I refined my guidance system until, eventually, I was no longer stuck. I was no longer in crisis, even as the world around me seemed to go ever deeper into it. I had found my way in life and know that I will never again be truly lost.

My desire to share this guidance system with you, to help you discover the most helpful direction *for you* in each moment, is what led me to create *Feel. Love. Now...*.

WHAT IS IT FOR?

Feel. Love. Now... is meant to offer you a reliable way to create wellness and stability in your life, regardless of which way and how hard the winds of change may blow. But, what does that really mean? What is stability when the entire world is changing so fast? What is wellness when there's so much illness in the world?

In an unstable environment, stability can only be relative. As everything is changing, it's no longer sensible to hold onto something and expect it to provide you with a firm foundation. It's as though the land beneath your feet that you used to feel was so safe to build on is now shifting, quaking, sinking, and erupting.

Stability is no longer something for you to seek outside yourself, because *your* stability is always relative to *you* – and no one else. This means that the stability you desire, to support you in building the life you wish to live, is *within* you. In an unstable world, stability is your ability to *rely on yourself*, your ability to support yourself, consistently. This is especially true when *everything* is changing, including yourself!

And, what about wellness? What does it even mean to be well – versus ill?

Wellness is an *increased ability* to function, while illness is a *decreased ability* to function. Wellness allows you to do more, more freely, while illness forces you to do less, with more restrictions and limitations. This means that wellness and illness are not specific to people or even to living beings. Wellness and illness are qualities of *everything that functions*, everything that is able to do something.

What *Feel. Love. Now...* is for is to provide you with a guidance system so that you can *rely on yourself* while also increasing the ability of *every aspect of your life* to function. This even includes increasing your *emotional wellness* so that you're able to live a life of true happiness.

WHO IS IT FOR?

The guidance system which *Feel. Love. Now...* helps you to create within yourself is something that I initially developed for myself. The understanding that it offers is one that I continue to find exceedingly useful in my life. The daily practices it describes are ones that I still practice. The questions it poses are ones that I continue to ask myself, fine-tuning my sense of direction.

When I first began to formulate the outline for *Feel. Love. Now...* in 2016, I assumed that it would be most helpful to men who were going through their midlife crisis, as I had. Yet, when I mentioned the intention for the book to much younger men, they often expressed a desire to read it. The more widely I spoke about it, the more widely I found people expressing great interest in it. It seemed that nearly everyone who was facing life's instability, regardless of age, sex, or social status, could see the value of having a reliable guidance system.

So, who is *Feel. Love. Now...* for? It's for *you*. The simple fact that you've reached this point suggests that you're aware of there being instability in some aspect of your life. You probably *know* that there are aspects of your life that feel unnecessarily restricted. You'd *appreciate* creating more wellness in your life. And, as a natural outcome, you may even desire to *feel love, now*, as well.

"Feel. Love. Now..." is not simply a title; it's also a way for you to easily remember how you can create stability and wellness within yourself in any given moment. To start with, *feel* your feelings – by giving attention to what you're experiencing. Then, *love* your life, including yourself, other people, and everything else you encounter.

No matter whether something is or isn't to your liking, you can still love it. So, if you find it confusing to love something that you don't like, simply offer your caring and compassion to everyone and everything you're experiencing – including yourself!

Feeling your feelings and loving your life can only be done *now*, not in the past and not in the future. If you try to feel and love your past, you're trying to love a memory rather than the life you're actually living. If you try to feel and love your future, you're trying to love a fantasy in place of the life you're actually living. *Now...* how can you feel love – now, to point you towards wellness and stability in each present moment?

How do I use it?

To construct your new guidance system and calibrate it to a life of wellness and stability, it's clearly helpful to have step-by-step instructions for both assembling and learning how to use it. So, that's what *Feel. Love. Now...* is designed to give you, in 3 sections over a period of 18 weeks.

If 18 weeks feels like a long time to you, that's wonderful – as you'll probably appreciate getting started right away! But, if you observe yourself being impatient, be sure to avoid skipping or rushing any steps.

You'll benefit most by building your new guidance system to be *accurate*. If you instead build it with pieces missing or even a few loose screws, it's the equivalent of building a compass that can't reliably point North.

For each weekly portion of the assembly instructions, you'll receive a lesson to deepen your *understanding* of yourself, a *practice* to train your body and self awareness, *questions* to deepen your self knowledge, and a weekly *review* to make sure you've mastered the material before continuing on to the next lesson. The practices for each week build on those of prior weeks and are to be done *daily*.

Introduction

Before you begin assembling please understand that, though each lesson is designed to be as simple and effective as possible, these lessons are probably *not* going to be easy for you! If you're at all like I was, there's probably a lot that you never knew you needed to know in order to live a life of stability and wellness. So, as you learn, please be kind and compassionate towards yourself. And, if it helps you to reread the lesson for a given week, even to reread it daily, please do!

Like all step-by-step instructions, the order of the steps is *meaningful* and the steps are meant to be followed in sequence. If you miss a day, extend the length of that "week" to cover the day that you missed so that you have 7 *days of practice* for each week of the program.

 If you simply aren't patient enough to wait 7 days before continuing to the next week's lesson, you may do one day's practice in the morning and another in the evening in order to have 2 days of practice in a single calendar day. However, I *strongly* recommend sticking to one day of practice for each day of the week in order to avoid feeling overwhelmed, no matter how many times per day you choose to practice.

If you feel an urge to skip portions of the practice, or to skip the practice altogether, *don't*. Each week's practice needs to be *practiced* for you to effectively use these instructions to create stability and wellness in your life. After all, it's not like you can build a guidance system merely by thinking about it!

The assembly instructions you'll be following are ones that I tested on myself *quite* thoroughly. Over the 18 months it took to develop *Feel. Love. Now...*, I purposefully created physical, emotional, mental, and spiritual instability in my own life by living in several dozen locations in 12 countries on 3 continents with no real income. Whenever I followed the instructions, my stability and wellness *increased*. Whenever I skipped or ignored any part of them, my stability and wellness *decreased*. It's truly that effective!

Each section of the guidance system requires 6 weeks to assemble and is associated with a different stage of the process. Section I focuses on how you're *feeling*, which is tied to your state of being. Section II focuses on how you're *loving*, which is tied to how you're doing. Section III focuses on how you're being present, which is tied to what you have present right *now*.

Like everyone else, you have physical, emotional, mental, and spiritual aspects. Because each of your aspects influences the others, the instructions in *Feel. Love. Now...* address them *together* rather than separately. This means that each lesson has physical, emotional, mental, and spiritual components, all of which are equally important.

Like everyone else, you are unique. This means that you differ from other people. And, while those differences do not make you *less* able to follow the steps for each practice, they do have an influence on *how* you will be able to follow them. Though adjustments and options are given as part of the description of the practices, you may need to further adjust one or more practices to address your specific needs, such as due to an injury. Remember, this is *your* new guidance system that you're building. So, be sure to follow the instructions in a way that allows *your* parts to fit together.

The most consistently significant difference that will influence the building of your new guidance system is your expression of gender.

Introduction

What this means is that your expression of masculinity and femininity, regardless of your genitalia, has a major influence on the directions you will choose to go in your life. So, to use these instructions, it's important for you to have a basic understanding of *both* femininity and masculinity. This is because both are always present in each of us, in different ways, and to varying degrees.

Femininity is the flowing, flowering fullness of life. It is the water-like quality of our reality that can flow like a river, sprinkle lightly, or be as deep and powerful as an ocean. Femininity is receptive, responsive, and reactive, while masculinity is penetrating, directed, and steady. Masculinity is the structure that gives form, direction, and support to the feminine flow of life.

Masculinity is like the banks of a river. Without its banks, a river's water would flood the land. With only a river's banks and no water, its riverbed would be lifeless. Both are needed and must *cooperate* in order for the rivers of life to thrive, within ourselves and in the world outside ourselves.

As *Feel. Love. Now...* was designed to provide you with form, direction, and support, it is highly masculine by nature. But, it does not assume that *you* are – or aren't. For your own masculinity, treat its structure as a type of scaffolding to help you build your own internal structures. For your own femininity, treat its structure as a system of channels and conduits to guide, accelerate, and focus your flow. As you feel into your truest expression of being, you will come to experience how this structure best serves you. So, let's begin!

Section I
FEEL.

Feel Your Sensations

UNDERSTANDING

The first step to creating wellness and stability in your life is to fully feel your sensations. Of course, you might think that you *are* fully feeling your sensations. After all, it's not like anyone else is feeling them for you. But, *how* fully are you feeling your sensations? Are you really giving them your full attention? Or, are you giving at least some of your attention to these words?

Because we can feel our own feelings whenever we give them our attention, it's easy to conclude that we know them. Yet, we don't necessarily *understand* them.

Fundamentally, your feelings are how you experience the feminine flow of life. This is true whether you're feeling your sensations, your emotions, your thoughts, or your creativity. In coming to *understand* your feelings, you are essentially creating a masculine structure within yourself to stabilize and support the feminine flow of your feelings.

YOU CAN UNDERSTAND YOUR FEELINGS TO BE THE FLOW OF INFORMATION *WITHIN YOUR BODY* THAT ALLOWS YOU TO PERCEIVE YOUR HUMAN EXISTENCE.

Since feelings are a flow of information, *feeling* your feelings is different than merely *having* feelings. This is because, in order to *feel* your feelings, you need to be *aware* of them. Whenever you're *not* aware of your feelings, the information they contain is unavailable to your conscious mind, as though you were partially under the influence of an anesthetic.

Since your feelings are a flow of information within your body, being *aware* of your feelings requires you to direct that flow of information *in on itself* as a sort of feedback loop. This means that feeling your feelings requires you to create a flow of information in your body (such as in your brain) *about* your body's flows of information.

The result of all this is that you must *choose* to feel your feelings fully in order to fully feel them. And, since this choice means that you're choosing how much to feel the flow of *life*, the degree to which you choose to feel your feelings is the degree to which you choose to *feel alive*.

So, let's start with your sensations. Because they're physical, your sensations allow you to feel the world around you. Or, at least that's what you likely *assume* to be true.

Your sensations arise from the stimulation of your physical senses, such as your eyesight, hearing, sense of taste, sense of touch, and every other physical sense that you're able to experience. This means that your sensory organs provide you with information based on how they sense the stimuli they receive from the physical world. However, this *doesn't* make them entirely accurate.

When was the last time you misheard something, misread something, or otherwise misidentified something you physically perceived? Knowing that, how likely is it that you've been misperceiving things but simply weren't aware of how *inaccurate* your perceptions were?

As it turns out, the answer is 100%. This is because, in order to be accurate, your perceptions need to correspond to the world outside yourself even though your perceptions are *feelings*, which are flows of information *within* your body.

Since your choices directly influence how your body functions, the way information flows within your body is affected by your choices. This means that *how* you choose to perceive has a tremendous influence on *what* you perceive, regardless of how your senses are stimulated. So, in simple terms, you can *never rely* on your perceptions to be entirely accurate.

Now you may be wondering, why is it so important to feel your sensations? After all, if you can't even rely on them to be accurate, what's the point in feeling them?

The reason that feeling your sensations is so important when it comes to creating wellness and stability in your life is that your sensations are what *connect* your physical being with the flow of life outside of yourself.

So, when you choose to avoid or minimize feeling your sensations, what you're doing is attempting to separate yourself from the rest of the world. Yet, that's simply not possible – because you're *a living part* of the world. This means that, whenever you attempt to avoid or minimize feeling your sensations, what you're doing is denying the fact that you're a living being, currently in the form of an animal known as a *human* being.

The reason you're even *able* to reduce the intensity of your sensations is that you're an animal. And we, over many millions of years of being animals, evolved the ability to avoid being overwhelmed by the intensity of our sensations when hurt. This ability was essential for us to survive being attacked by predators, for example. Otherwise, if a predator bit your hand, you wouldn't be able to run to safety because you'd be overwhelmed by the pain in your hand!

When you minimize feeling sensations in your daily life, what you're doing is attempting to protect yourself from being overwhelmed by *potential harm.* Yet, since in reality attempting to protect yourself from potential harm *limits and prevents you* from doing other things, feeling your sensations as fully as possible *frees you* to fully live your real life.

The freedom to live your life fully allows you the freedom to be fully well, which makes it even more enjoyable to feel the fullness of your life! Still, should you ever feel overwhelmed, the freedom to live your life also allows you the freedom to *reduce* the intensity of your sensations. Truly, it's a no-lose proposition! So, let's practice feeling those sensations.

PRACTICE

The daily practice you'll be using to construct your internal guidance system is designed to gradually train your body, heart, mind, and spirit to feel more fully, love more fully, and be more present. Day by day and week by week, your daily practice will support you in creating stability and wellness in your life. So, be sure to take as much time as you need for it.

Each week, instructions will be provided for you to extend your practice from the week before, indicating a goal to achieve, a breathing exercise, a movement exercise, a summary of steps to follow, and an indication of what to focus on *beyond* the exercises.

While it may seem that there are a lot of instructions here, you'll know that you're succeeding whenever you achieve your goal for the week. The rest of the instructions are provided to support you in making your daily practice more refined and more effective.

Goal

The goal for this week is to relax, stand up straight, and feel your sensations.

Breath

The key to achieving your goal rests in your breath. So, begin by breathing deeply with an open mouth. It doesn't matter how wide you keep your mouth open but be sure to keep the tip of your tongue pressed lightly to the roof of your mouth. It's fine if you need to close your mouth to swallow; just open your mouth back up afterwards to continue breathing as before. There's no need to breathe through your nose at this point, as nasal congestion can cause your air intake to be inconsistent over the duration of the program.

Breathe in deeply, extending your belly downwards and only then expanding your chest. Breathe out deeply, pulling your belly towards your spine and only *then* contracting your chest gently.

Keep the duration of your in-breaths and out-breaths long and even, without creating any shallowness in your breath. To help you maintain evenness and consistency, occupy your mind with the following words as you inhale:

I am healthy.

I am wealthy.

I am blessed.

I am loved.

Begin to silently think the words when you begin to inhale and complete the last word at the end of each inhalation. Transition smoothly from inhalation to exhalation to avoid holding your breath. As you exhale, occupy your mind with *these* words:

Yes!

I am grateful!

Thank you, Source!

1

As with your inhalation, begin to silently think the words when you begin to exhale and complete the last word at the end of your exhalation. Replace the 1 with the count of each breath, such as 2, 3, and so on.

Transition smoothly from exhalation to inhalation in order to avoid holding your breath at any point during the practice. This exercise is about breathing deeply, not quickly. So, keep it nice and slow.

THIS BREATHING EXERCISE IS THE *MOST IMPORTANT* ELEMENT OF THE ENTIRE PROGRAM. SO, TAKE AS MUCH TIME AS YOU NEED TO IN ORDER TO MASTER IT!

The meaning of the words you'll be telling yourself is *very* important. So, let's clarify them. For the inhalation:

I am healthy.

I am wealthy.

I am blessed.

I am loved.

Even though I may not know you personally, I know that each of these statements about you is *true*, whenever you acknowledge them. This is because, no matter how ill or injured you are, you always have *some* health. Otherwise, you wouldn't be alive to understand these words!

No matter how poor or indebted you are, you always have *some* wealth. It may not be financial but you still have wealth in your relationships, in your community, and in Nature, for example.

No matter how hurt or abused you may be, there are always *some* blessings in your life. If you ever feel called to keep yourself busy, simply count your blessings!

No matter how ignored or unappreciated you may be, you are always receiving *some* love, even when it's not in the ways that you may prefer. After all, your Mother Earth loves you enough to provide you with air to breathe, sunlight to see, water to drink, and food to eat.

So, yes, you *are* healthy. You *are* wealthy. You are both blessed *and* loved. Isn't that wonderful?! Isn't that something to treasure and be grateful for? So, the meanings of the words on your exhalation now become clearer:

Yes!

I am grateful!

Thank you, Source!

1

"Yes!" affirms the *truth* of how wonderful your life actually is, regardless of your challenges and your disappointments. "I am grateful!" affirms your gratitude to be *alive* and to experience being *you.* "Thank you, Source!" expresses that gratitude to the *ultimate source* of all existence, regardless of any beliefs you may have about that source. And, the count of breaths at the end acts as a tracking device for you to stay focused and avoid drifting off too far from the practice.

When it comes to the meanings of words, your intention and expression matter *more* than any definition in the dictionary. After all, how many ways can you say the word "yes"? How many *meanings* can you convey with that one word, alone?

So, now that you understand the meanings of the words that you'll be thinking to yourself as part of the breathing exercise, align your *intentions* and your *expression* of those words with their intended meaning. Allow yourself to be sincere, because it is only through aligning your intention with your expression that you give your words power.

There's no reason to hold back and be shy about it. After all, you're saying these words *to yourself*. Plus, you're not even saying them out loud! So, raise your internal volume, sing them boldly if you wish, and *breathe deeply*.

Movement

Once you've learned how to breathe for the purposes of this practice, you can begin the first step of your movement exercise by being barefoot and standing up straight on a level surface, with your eyes open. Look straight ahead, at the level of the horizon, and gently gaze on whatever you see before you that isn't moving.

To stand up *straight*, you can imagine a string attached to the crown of your head, tugging you up to the sky, while a weight attached to your tailbone tugs you down towards the ground. The crown of your head is the point where your spine would poke out from the top of your head if it kept going straight up from the back of your neck through your skull. This combination of tension and relaxation will naturally result in your chin coming to rest near your throat as you stand.

FEEL. LOVE. NOW...

Balance your weight at the top of the *arches* of your feet, halfway between the ball and heel of each foot. Have your feet pointed *forward*, as though the toe closest to your big toe was an arrow pointing straight ahead of you. You will likely feel pressure on the ball, heel, and outer edge of your feet but not the arches themselves.

If your feet feel flat on the floor, turn your hips outward and pivot your feet to point forward once more. You can make sure that your feet are directly under your hips by having your arms pointing *straight down* at your sides before you begin, with your legs lightly touching the palms of your hands. Be sure to avoid locking your knees at any point during your practice.

On the *first* inhalation of your movement exercise, raise your arms from your sides so that the palms of your hands meet high above your head. On your first *exhalation*, lower your hands together, in "prayer pose", so that you press your palms together gently in front of your heart. Simply stand there with your hands in front of your heart and breathe for a count of 10 breaths, using the instructions for your breathing exercise.

While standing, relax your body by letting go of any tension that isn't required for you to remain standing straight. For example, are you holding tension in your jaw, your shoulders, your abdomen, or your anus that isn't actually helping you to stand up straight?

If any thoughts arise, other than the words you're telling yourself as part of the breathing exercise, observe them as though they were passing clouds. Let go of any need to follow them or hold onto them. Instead, *feel your sensations* by turning your attention towards your *body,* as you scan it to see which parts you can relax even further while continuing to stand up straight.

Steps

	FOCUS	MOVEMENT	BREATH
1	Feel your sensations	Standing straight	Stage 1

Beyond

Be sure to do this practice *every day,* for 7 days, before you start Week 2. As you train yourself to feel your sensations more and more, allow yourself to feel your sensations more fully *outside* of the practice. And, if you ever feel distressed at any point during the week, simply practice your breathing exercise until you feel more at ease. You'll discover the difference to be quite remarkable!

QUESTIONS

Every day, after you do the practice portion of this week's lesson, ask yourself these questions. Answer them with the *first* response that comes to your mind to discover what is true for you in that moment. If you find yourself trying to analyze the questions instead of simply answering them, relax your mind and notice the *way* that you're thinking.

- How does it feel to breathe deeply, in comparison with having shallow breaths?

- Are you feeling the excitement of curiosity as you learn this week's lesson?

- Are you feeling any fears as you learn this week's lesson?

- How easy is it for you to relax your body while standing up straight?

- Are you trying to "get it right"?

- Are you judging yourself unkindly when your actions don't precisely match the instructions?

- Do you feel more stable than you did before you began today's practice?

- Do you feel freer or more restricted after today's practice?

- How "loud" and energized can you be when expressing the meanings of the words that you were thinking to yourself, as part of the practice?

- Did you find yourself smiling during the practice and, if not, why not?

- Have you been sitting up and standing up straight throughout your day and, if not, why not?

- Have you been feeling your sensations today more than yesterday?

REVIEW

Although each week's Understanding offers useful information to contemplate, much of what you learn from this program will be the result of *doing* your Practice daily, *answering* each week's list of Questions daily, and *applying* each week's lesson to your daily life.

So on the *seventh day*, after answering the list of Questions, see how much you've mastered this week's lesson by observing whether you've come to realize or understand these key insights:

* ✳ Feelings are the flow of information *within* your body that allows you to perceive your human existence.

* ✳ Your *perceptions* of what's outside of you are not entirely accurate because perceptions are feelings, which are flows of information *inside* of you.

* ✳ Your *sensations* are feelings that connect your physical being with the feminine flow of life.

* ✳ *Understanding* creates masculine structure to support the flow of your feelings.

* ✳ Feeling your physical being is *necessary* for you to be physically well.

* ✳ Feeling your sensations allows you to *attend* to your body's well-being.

* ✳ Feeling your feelings requires you to be *aware* of your feelings.

* ✳ Feelings exist for you to *feel* them.

✳ Expanding your capacity to feel requires *discipline.*

✳ Coming to *understand* your feelings requires discipline.

✳ How strongly you feel your feelings determines how strongly you feel *alive.*

✳ To minimize feeling your sensations is to *constrain* yourself in an attempt to avoid pain.

✳ Pain *signals* potential harm.

✳ Seeking to *avoid* feeling is aspiring towards death.

✳ Feeling your sensations as fully as possible *frees you* to fully live your real life.

✳ Fully living your life isn't always pleasant but it is *necessary* in order to be well.

✳ The freedom to fully live your life allows you the *freedom* to be fully well.

✳ Stability is available *inside of you* regardless of what's happening outside of you.

✳ The feminine flow of feeling is what *nourishes and enlivens* you.

✳ The masculine structure of understanding is what *supports and stabilizes* you.

✳ Relaxation *helps you* to both feel and be stable.

✳ Breathing *deeply and evenly* helps you to relax.

✳ Standing straight and sitting straight help you to *breathe* more deeply.

✳ Accepting your sensations requires you to accept your *body*.

✳ Accepting your body requires you to accept that you're an *animal*.

✳ You can choose to feel your sensations *less* when you need to protect yourself from being overwhelmed.

✳ It's rare for you to *need* to protect yourself from being overwhelmed.

✳ Rather than choosing to feel less, you can exercise your breathing to increase your *stability*.

✳ Aligning your intention with your expression is what gives *power* to your words.

✳ You are responsible for *choosing* what you give power to and how much power you give.

✳ Your ability to direct your own power is the *foundation* of your stability and wellness.

✳ It's easy to hold *tension* in ways that don't serve your wellness.

✳ It can be surprisingly challenging to stand up straight for 10 deep breaths and *not* think.

✳ Judging yourself *doesn't* help you to learn.

✳ Learning to *be* well is learning to *live* well.

✳ Allow yourself to be *grateful* that you're able to feel.

✳ The only thing you need to *do* with your feelings is feel them.

✳ You are *blessed* to be alive.

✳ Relaxation is *key*.

✳ Relax and *learn* while loving each moment.

Feel Your Emotions

UNDERSTANDING

When you did your daily practice and asked yourself the questions for Week 1, you may have noticed some feelings arising. If so, great job! You overachiever... You were feeling your emotions, which is the focus of this week's lesson. But, what *are* emotions and what purpose do they serve?

Because an emotion is a type of feeling, you know from last week's lesson that emotions are part of the flow of information within your body that allows you to perceive your human existence. However, emotions differ from sensations.

As you might remember, sensations are feelings that allow you to perceive things about the environment *outside* your sense of self, through the stimulation of your physical senses. In comparison, emotions are feelings that allow you to perceive things about the environment *inside* your sense of self, through the state of your nervous system. But, what does that mean?

Your sense of self is what you use to distinguish what is you from what is not you, while your nervous system is what allows your body to feel, think, and create. Your nervous system includes your brain, spinal cord, sensory organs, nerves (not surprisingly), and every other part of your body that allows you to perceive life as a human being. This even includes portions of your heart and gut.

BY ALLOWING YOU TO FEEL THE *STATE* OF YOUR NERVOUS SYSTEM, EMOTIONS ALLOW YOU TO BECOME *AWARE* OF THE THOUGHTS AND BELIEFS YOU HAVE ABOUT YOUR SENSE OF SELF.

Like everyone else, you experience *two* primary types of emotions, *expansive* ones and *contractive* ones. We'll refer to them that way because, while expansive emotions indicate the *expanded* state of your nervous system, contractive emotions indicate the *contracted* state of your nervous system.

The more expanded your nervous system is, the more *open* you are to supporting the flow of life beyond your sense of self. The more contracted your nervous system is, the more *closed* you are to supporting the flow of life beyond your sense of self. This means that you have both a *range* of emotion, based on *how much* contraction you're experiencing in your nervous system, and a *complexity* of emotion, based on which *parts* of your nervous system are contracting or expanding.

Each degree of emotional contraction or expansion that you feel can be useful in specific situations, related to how we evolved as animals. So, there's a lot to learn from them – and about them!

As animals, we evolved to have contractive emotions so as to *unconsciously* stay alive by *maintaining* our sense of self. This is why contractive emotions urge you to either *withdraw* inwards or *seek* outwards. Since withdrawing from the flow of life closes you from it more than seeking outside yourself, contractive-withdrawing emotions are *more* contracted than contractive-seeking ones.

Your contractive-withdrawing emotions help you to maintain your survival by directing you to avoid *potential* threats. By avoiding the *possibility* of real danger, you are more likely to stay alive. Contractive-withdrawing emotions can be distinguished as having 3 types. These types direct you to withdraw when you are *overcome by your feelings*, when you *lack desired support*, and when you *perceive danger*.

Contractive emotions that direct you to withdraw when you are overcome or overwhelmed are the *most* contractive ones. Examples include *despair, apathy,* and *boredom*. These emotions are useful to you when you're overwhelmed by your feelings, to the point of not being able to function effectively while feeling your experience fully. By withdrawing your awareness away from your *being*, you're then able to focus your awareness on whatever you're *doing* and avoid losing your sense of self in the midst of your discomfort.

The *next* most contractive emotions are ones that direct you to withdraw when you lack the support you desire. Examples include *sadness, regret,* and *shame*. These emotions are useful to you in cases when you're better off *partially withdrawing* from life, allowing you to conserve your energy when you're not able to receive the support you need to function at your fullest.

Contractive emotions that direct you to withdraw when perceiving danger are the *least* contractive of the contractive-withdrawing emotions. Examples include *fear, disgust,* and *panic.* These emotions are useful when you're faced with a threat to your ability to function and need to withdraw in order to protect yourself from harm or injury.

As animals, we evolved contractive-seeking emotions to direct us in *seeking* the resources we need in order to maintain our sense of self. As a social animal, some of the most important resources you can have are *social* resources, things like *attention, affection, appreciation, admiration,* and *acceptance.*

Contractive-seeking emotions exist to unconsciously direct you to seek resources *for yourself.* Similar to contractive-withdrawing emotions, there are 3 types of contractive-seeking emotions. These types direct you to *seek out* resources, *seek the redistribution* of resources, and *seek to receive* resources.

The most contractive of your contractive-seeking emotions are ones which urge you to seek *out* resources. Examples include *want, anticipation,* and *envy.* These emotions are useful when some action is required for you to gain access to a needed resource that is not immediately available to you in order to maintain your sense of self.

The next most contractive of your contractive-seeking emotions are ones which urge you to seek the *redistribution of resources.* Examples include *anger, jealousy,* and *resentment.* These emotions are useful when you're not receiving enough resources, including social resources, and action is required for you to ensure that you receive an adequate share in order to maintain your sense of self.

The least contractive of your contractive-seeking emotions are ones which urge you to seek to *receive* resources. Examples include *pride, arrogance,* and *self-righteousness.* These emotions are useful when others are *excluding* you from receiving resources and action is required to show them that you are worthy of being *included* in receiving resources in order to maintain your sense of self.

Fundamentally, contractive-seeking emotions direct you to seek resources due to *beliefs of insufficiency.* In other words, your contractive-seeking emotions reveal that a part of you is afraid that you *do not* or *will not* have enough resources to maintain your sense of self.

While contractive-seeking emotions are not as energetically draining as contractive-withdrawing emotions, emotions are energetically draining *in proportion* to how contractive they are. This means that it is more draining to feel want than to feel anger and less draining to feel pride than to feel either resentment or envy. This is why people often choose to feel more energized by expressing anger or arrogance than to be vulnerable enough to admit that they feel sad or afraid.

Your emotional wellness is determined by how *expansively* you allow yourself to feel your emotions. Because of how your nervous system contracts and expands to limit or free the flow of your feelings, expanding your emotional state is similar to freeing the flow of water in a hose. For instance, you might *dissolve blockages* in the hose, *soften the resistance* of the hose, or *increase the flow* of water in the hose. Similarly, expanding your emotional state frees the flow of your feelings in support of the flow of life.

Your least expansive emotions are ones which urge you to *dissolve blockages* to the flow of life. Examples include *courage, confidence,* and *curiosity.* These emotions are useful when some action is required for you to release whatever is in the way of the free flow of life.

Your next most expansive emotions are ones which urge you to *soften resistance* to the flow of life. Examples include *caring, acceptance,* and *playfulness.* These emotions are useful when you have things to share and some action is required for you to lessen your resistance to sharing them in order to support the flow of life.

Your *most* expansive emotions are ones which urge you to *increase the flow* of life. Examples include feelings of *gratitude, freedom,* and *oneness.* These emotions are useful when some action is required for you to maintain and expand your openness to supporting the flow of life.

Since living well is fundamentally about increasing the ability of life to function, following the guidance of your expansive emotions helps you to live well by helping *life* to live well. This is why *joy, delight,* and *wonder* are all expansive emotions and why wellness is and feels *joyful, delightful,* and *wonderful.*

In summary, basic emotions range from most expansive to most contractive:

EXPANSIVE EMOTIONS - SUPPORT THE FLOW OF LIFE

Gratitude, Freedom, Oneness - Increase Flow

Caring, Acceptance, Playfulness - Soften Resistance

Courage, Confidence, Curiosity - Dissolve Blockages

CONTRACTIVE EMOTIONS - MAINTAIN SENSE OF SELF

Contractive-Seeking Emotions - Seek Outwards to Maintain Sense of Self

Pride, Arrogance, Self-Righteousness - Seek to Receive Resources

Anger, Jealousy, Resentment - Seek to Redistribute Resources

Want, Anticipation, Envy - Seek Out Resources

Contractive-Withdrawing Emotions - Withdraw to Maintain Sense of Self

Fear, Disgust, Panic - When Perceiving Danger

Sadness, Regret, Shame - When Lacking Desired Support

Despair, Apathy, Boredom - When Overcome by Feelings

The summary above doesn't include complex emotional states, such as feeling hatred or feeling overcome with regret. This is because complex emotional states combine basic emotional states in different parts of your nervous system. Also, the summary doesn't include happiness because happiness isn't really an emotion. Instead, happiness is your openness to *feeling* your emotions.

Joy, an expansive emotion related to feelings of gratitude, freedom, and oneness, has commonly been *confused* with happiness. Presumably, this confusion is related to the fact that you can *only* feel joy when you're entirely happy. Yet, you *can* be happy *without* feeling joy.

When you limit your openness to feeling your emotions, you do so by *contracting*. So really, you can only limit the *expansiveness* of the state of your nervous system. This means that the most expansive emotions are the *first* ones you close yourself off from, whenever you're less open to feeling your emotions.

The more closed off you are to feeling your emotions, the more limited you are to feeling only the more contractive ones. This means that happiness allows you to feel joy while also *requiring you* to feel any fear, sadness, or despair in your nervous system. Essentially, complete happiness is when you open yourself to *fully and freely* feel your emotions.

Understanding emotions, both yours and others', is an incredibly powerful way to create stability and wellness in your life! So, feel free to refer back to this week's lesson whenever you suppose a review might be helpful.

As you look over the list, you might notice that the range of emotions you just learned has some similarities to other terminology you may have heard before, such as light to dark, love to fear, positive to negative, or light to heavy. However, there are no *bad* emotions. Emotions are simply feelings that provide you with *urges* that are only useful to follow in *specific* situations to maintain your sense of self or support the flow of life.

When you understand your emotions, it allows you to understand the messages that your nervous system is communicating to you and others, both consciously and subconsciously. Understanding emotions also allows you to understand the messages that *other* people are subconsciously communicating, both to you and to themselves.

For example, if you're angry, what is it that you feel you're not getting enough of? Are you seen as not getting enough from *multiple* perspectives or just your own?

If someone is afraid, what danger is that person perceiving to their sense of self? Is the perceived danger a real threat to them? If not, what can you do to ease their fears by showing them that they're safe?

From what you've learned here, you can understand emotions to be feelings in the form of urges that are based on the *stories* that people have about themselves. Because these stories of selfhood only represent a single perspective, though, they're inherently incomplete and often inaccurate. That's why it often *isn't* useful to follow the urges of your emotions. However, it's always useful to *listen* to the messages your emotions are telling you about yourself *without* reacting to them. And, the same is true for the emotions of other people.

WHEN YOU FULLY FEEL YOUR EMOTIONS
WITHOUT REACTING TO THEM,
YOU BECOME MORE *STABLE* WITHIN YOURSELF.
WHEN YOU'RE NO LONGER REACTING TO YOUR FEELINGS,
YOU ARE TRULY *FREE* TO BE THE PERSON
YOU CHOOSE TO BE.

Understanding your emotions and the emotions of others allows you to respond with *love* instead of reacting based on your prior assumptions. As for how, we'll get to that in Section II. In the meantime, though, *fully feel your emotions* without reacting to them and you will soon discover more stability, wellness, and happiness in your life.

PRACTICE

To begin your daily practice for Week 2, start by doing the first step of your daily practice as you learned it for Week 1. Then, once you've completed the first step, begin Step 2 by adding a new layer to your breathing exercise.

Goal

The goal for this week is to relax, fold forward, and feel your emotions.

Breath

For Stage 2 of your breathing exercise, add onto what you learned in Week 1 by allowing yourself to expand your emotional state from most contracted to least contracted every time you inhale. This means that, when you start inhaling, you'll allow yourself to feel despair, apathy, boredom, or any other state of being emotionally overcome. By the time you finish inhaling, you'll have expanded your emotional state to feel pride, arrogance, self-righteousness, or any other emotion that urges you to seek to receive resources.

To make it easier for you, you can time the expansion of your emotional state with the words that you're thinking to yourself. So, when you begin to think "I am healthy" you can start to feel overcome, such as feeling *despair*. By the time you finish thinking to yourself that "I am wealthy", you'll be feeling a sense of danger, such as feeling *fear*. As you start to think "I am blessed", you'll be feeling an urge to seek out resources, such as feeling *want*. And by the time you finish thinking "I am loved", you'll be feeling an urge to seek to receive resources, such as feeling *pride*.

Every time you exhale, allow yourself to expand your emotional state further from least expanded to most expanded. This means that, when you start exhaling, you'll allow yourself to feel courage, confidence, curiosity, or any other state that dissolves blockages to the flow of life. By the time you finish exhaling, you'll have expanded your emotional state to feel gratitude, freedom, oneness, or any other joyful state that increases the flow of life.

To make it easier for you, you can further time the expansion of your emotional state with the words you're thinking to yourself. When you begin to think "Yes!", you can start to dissolve any blockages that you may have to supporting the flow of life, such as feeling *courage*. When you think "I am grateful!", you can soften any resistance you may have to supporting the flow of life, such as feeling *acceptance*. When you think "Thank you, Source!", you can increase the flow of life within yourself, such as feeling *gratitude*. And, as you think of the current count, you can linger there.

Of course, it can be difficult at first for you to consciously contract and expand your emotions in this way. So, it may help you to "act it out" as though you were auditioning for a play. If you do, you'll likely notice that great actors are able to act so well because of how well they're able to create the emotions they express in their performances. Have you noticed that you can feel how authentic a person is when they express their feelings?

Assuming you're not a professional actor, though, training yourself to contract and expand your nervous system along with everything else these practices call for is likely to be challenging for you. So, it may help you to think of this process as similar to learning a foreign language. The same way that it's not reasonable to assume that you'll become fluent in a foreign language overnight, the practices in *Feel. Love. Now...* require *practice.*

As you follow the instructions to the best of your ability, observe how you *learn and improve* with practice. If the practice during a particular breath was particularly challenging for you, you can repeat the count of that breath the same way that you might repeat the pronunciation of an especially difficult phrase in a foreign language. However, it's best that you avoid stopping and restarting the practice in an attempt to get things perfect.

As you continue to make progress in your practice, remember that you are training your nervous system to create *wellness and stability* in your life.

This is definitely a language worth learning!

Movement

Once you've completed your initial 10 breaths while standing straight for Step 1, you'll begin Step 2 of your movement exercise by resetting your count of breaths to 1 and beginning Stage 2 of your breathing exercise. As you begin Step 2 of your movement exercise, maintain your standing posture and bring your palms together high above your head as you inhale.

As you exhale, fold forward, sweep your arms outward and bring your hands to touch opposite elbows with your arms hanging down. Be sure to maintain a straight back by bending *only* at your waist. This means that you might not be bending forward very far, which is fine.

Be sure to stop bending once you've gone 4% past your edge of discomfort. This means that this portion of your movement exercise won't be comfortable – but it won't be painful either. Keep your head aligned with your straight back, rather than letting it hang down.

On your inhalation, bring yourself back to standing as you sweep your arms outward, bringing your palms together high above your head. Once you've returned to standing upright, make sure to keep your head level by following the instructions you received for Week 1 on how to stand up straight.

Because you'll be sweeping your arms outward on both your inhalation and exhalation, be sure to have enough space to do so without hitting anything. If the room you have available for your practice is too confining, you can substitute sweeping your arms outward by sweeping them *forward*.

As you move your arms and torso, let your *breaths* lead your movements, rather than breathing in *response* to your movement. Remember, the breathing exercise is the *most important* part of the program. So, maintain your updated breathing exercise as you continue this portion of your movement exercise for 10 breaths. This means that you will be feeling your emotional range *in addition to* maintaining the breathing exercise you learned for Week 1.

As there are two ways to hold opposite elbows, depending on which arm is forward, alternate between them with each breath. Keep feeling and relaxing into your edge of discomfort, noticing how it changes, and adjust your movements to go just 4% past your edge. Be sure to notice if your edge of discomfort is actually more emotional than physical!

Although you might find yourself stretching a bit, stretching is *not* the point of the practice. Instead, the point of this portion of your movement exercise is to *relax and open* into fully feeling your emotions and sensations, even in the midst of your discomfort. As you do so, you may notice that your movement and emotions are influencing your breathing. If that's the case, see if you can maintain the same pace and depth of breath that you had while you were standing straight for Step 1.

You might notice your clothes getting in the way of your free movement. So, starting this week, be sure to wear clothing that allows your body to move freely. It will definitely be helpful later!

This exercise may bring up a lot of stories for you, which is perfectly fine. Simply feel and observe them without reacting or attaching to them. See them fly by you like passing birds. And, if they land close by and start chirping away, don't bother having a conversation with them. Instead, just hear what's being expressed the same way that you'd hear some birds chirping nearby and let them fly away whenever they like.

Steps

	FOCUS	MOVEMENT	BREATH
1	Feel your sensations	Standing straight	Stage 1
2	Feel your emotions	Forward Folding	Stage 2

Beyond

Be sure to do this practice *every day*, for 7 days, before you start Week 3. As you train yourself to feel your emotional range more and more, allow yourself to *fully feel* both your sensations and your emotions *outside* of the practice.

IF YOU EVER FEEL STRESSED AT ANY POINT
THROUGHOUT YOUR DAY, SIMPLY AND GENTLY DO
YOUR UPDATED BREATHING EXERCISE
AND REMEMBER TO "FEEL. LOVE. NOW..."

In case you feel an urge to express your emotions *and* you're in a safe environment to do so, please do! This may involve crying, stomping, or even screaming. As long as you are feeling your emotions fully and releasing them, rather than attaching and reacting to them, it will be like liberating birds from their cages.

QUESTIONS

Every day, after you do the practice portion of this week's lesson, ask yourself these questions and discover what answers are true for you in the moment.

- Were you bending your knees to make it easier to fold forward further?

- Were you so focused on following the instructions that you forgot to feel your sensations and emotions?

- Were you so distracted by your feelings that you forgot to follow the instructions?

- When you were bending forward, did it feel more stable for you to close your eyes or keep them open?

- Did you start to get off balance when you were folding forward?

- Did you lose track of the breathing exercise at any point during the practice?

- Did you judge the practice as being too hard or judge yourself for not having mastered it yet?

- Are you reacting to your emotions less than you did before today's practice?

- Are you feeling more stable and at peace than you were before today's practice?

FEEL. LOVE. NOW...

- Are you feeling more free to be you than you were before today's practice and, if not, what's getting in the way of that?

- Have you been feeling your emotions today more than yesterday?

REVIEW

After answering the list of Questions on the *seventh day*, see how much you've mastered this week's lesson by observing whether you've come to realize or understand these key insights:

* Emotions are feelings that allow you to perceive things about the environment *inside* your sense of self.

* Your sense of self is what you use to *distinguish* what is you from what is not you.

* Though you *experience* emotions, you are not your emotions.

* Emotions do not happen to you; you create them with your *stories*.

* Your *nervous system* is what allows your body to feel, think, and create.

* Thinking is optional; *feeling* is not.

* Coming to *understand* your feelings requires discipline.

* Understanding directs the flow of *information* in your nervous system.

* To *understand* your emotions is to understand the messages your nervous system is communicating both to you and others.

* Emotions have a *range* from most contractive to most expansive.

* *Contractive* emotions exist to maintain your sense of self.

✳ Contractive emotions *urge you* to either withdraw inwards or seek outwards.

✳ Contractive emotions arise from beliefs that your sense of self is being *threatened*.

✳ *Expansive* emotions exist to support the flow of life.

✳ Expansive emotions urge you to *encourage, welcome, and intensify* the flow of life.

✳ Expansive emotions come from knowing that you are *one* with the flow of life.

✳ The more contractive an emotion is, the more *draining* it feels.

✳ The more expansive an emotion is, the more *energizing* it feels.

✳ The more contractive an emotion is, the more *tense* you feel.

✳ The more expansive an emotion is, the more *relaxed* you feel.

✳ The emotions you feel and the emotions you *desire to feel* may differ.

✳ Emotions need to be felt, *not* overcome.

✳ Expanding your capacity to feel requires *discipline*.

✳ Happiness is when you *open* yourself to fully and freely feel your emotions.

✳ Happiness is a state of emotional *wellness*.

✳ Emotional wellness is emotional *freedom*.

* Contractive emotions *urge you* to limit your freedom.

* In addition to range and complexity, emotions vary in *intensity*.

* The more intensely expansive an emotion is, the more *enjoyable* it is.

* When you feel your emotions without reacting to them, you become more *stable*.

* Emotions of the same type differ based on the *stories* you have about them.

* You are able to *create, influence, and direct* your emotions through your stories.

* Great acting is the result of the actors' great skill in *creating* their emotions.

* Your ability to *regulate* your emotional responses determines your emotional stability.

* Emotional regulation is *essential* for your wellness.

* You are *responsible* for your emotions.

* You become emotionally *unstable* by leaving your emotions unregulated.

* You leave your emotions *unregulated* by suppressing, repressing, denying, distracting, or projecting them.

* Emotions are *not* directives.

✳ Accepting your emotions is necessary to accept *yourself* in each moment.

✳ To accept yourself, *release* all shame, guilt, and insecurity.

✳ Accepting your emotions allows you to lovingly *attend* to those aspects of yourself that you may not have been aware of otherwise.

✳ To maintain your sense of self is to *minimize* changes to who you are.

✳ Creating a life of stability and wellness may require *substantial* changes.

✳ Emotional *pain* signals a perceived threat to your sense of self.

✳ You can experience *very intense* contractive emotions when creating a life of stability and wellness.

✳ You contract your nervous system to *reduce* the intensity of your feelings.

✳ Feeling contractive emotions *without* contracting your nervous system requires you to feel them fully.

✳ Emotion is how the process of resolving your stories *feels* in your nervous system.

✳ No emotion is *inherently* good or bad, harmful or helpful.

✳ How you *behave* in response to your emotions may be either harmful or helpful.

✳ Emotional urges are only useful to follow in *specific* situations.

✳ Following your emotions instead of regulating them *prevents you* from leading a life of wellness.

✳ You need to *feel* your emotions in order to regulate them.

✳ Feel and release your *resistance* in each moment.

✳ Relaxation is *key*.

✳ Relax and *learn* while loving each moment.

Feel Your Cycles

UNDERSTANDING

Breathing in – and breathing out, it's one of the fundamental cycles that powers us as living beings. Day and night, Winter and Summer, growth and decay, the ebb and the flow... Cycles are the basis of all life.

TO RESIST THE CYCLES OF YOUR LIFE IS TO RESIST THE BASIS OF YOUR BEING *ALIVE*.

The Sun will set and the Sun will rise. You are not here on this Earth to change that. Neither are you here to ignore it. Instead, the more aware you are of the cycles of life, the more aware you are of life itself.

It is the nature of our existence that, in order for there to be more, there must also be less. If there was no such thing as less, there could be no such thing as more because there would be no way to compare. This aspect of our existence is known as polarity, also sometimes referred to as duality.

It is the polar, or dualistic, nature of your existence that allows for your range of emotions to go from contracted to expanded. It's what allows you to distinguish pain from pleasure and judge things as better or worse.

POLARITY IS NECESSARY FOR CYCLES TO EXIST BECAUSE CYCLES ARE THE *DYNAMIC BALANCING* OF THINGS THAT ARE IN OPPOSITION TO ONE ANOTHER.

It's like the swing of a pendulum going across a center line, moving back and forth between left and right. For there to be highs, there must be lows – and vice versa. The less you feel the lows in your life, the less you're able to appreciate the highs. It's only when you feel the *full range* of your experience that you are able to live a full life of wellness. So, feel the cycles of your life in their fullness!

Feel how hungry or full you are. Feel how thirsty or sated you are. Feel how clean or dirty you are. Are you feeling tired? Are you feeling rested? Are you feeling energized?

Your feelings are what give you the information you require in order to take care of yourself, no matter how ill or well you may feel. At any given moment, knowing where you are in the cycles of your life helps you in adjusting your actions to better support your wellness.

Are you eating when you're not actually hungry, drinking when you're not actually thirsty, washing when you're not actually dirty, and resting when you're not actually tired?

Are you *not* eating when you're actually hungry, *not* drinking when you're actually thirsty, *not* washing when you're actually dirty, and *not* resting when you're actually tired?

THE MORE YOU FEEL THE CYCLES OF LIFE, THE MORE THEY INFORM YOU ABOUT WHAT IS *USEFUL* AND WHAT IS *NOT USEFUL* FOR YOU TO ATTEND TO.

Since you're easily able to form habits, it's easy for you to do something *entirely* out of habit instead of acting consciously. Where habit would have you act based on the past, acting consciously requires you to respond to what you're feeling *in the present moment.*

Habits allow you to conserve your energy by *not focusing your awareness* on things that you're already familiar with. Because being aware requires you to use your body's energy reserves, it's by *limiting* your awareness that you're able to conserve your energy. And, it's by limiting your awareness that you become *unconscious* of the life you're actually living.

Though habits offer you familiarity, they *don't* offer you stability. If you have a habit of veering left and decide to walk along a balance beam, your habit will help to *destabilize* you. If something bumps into the balance beam, even a habit of walking in a straight line can help to destabilize you.

FEEL. LOVE. NOW...

INSTEAD OF RELYING ON WHAT YOU'VE DONE IN THE PAST, IT IS UP TO YOU TO FEEL FULLY INTO *EACH MOMENT*.

Fully feeling each moment allows you to create stability as a conscious response to whatever is present for you. Of course this means that you'll be using more of your energy reserves but, as long as you're eating enough, you'll find that being more conscious *actively benefits* your body and substantially increases your wellness in every aspect of your life.

When you feel the cycles of your life, you become *more conscious* of the life you're living. Then, as you become more conscious of your life, you enable yourself to let go of old habits whenever you decide to do so.

The freer you are of your habits, the freer you are in your life. The freer you are to make choices, the freer you are to *direct* your life. The freer you are in directing your focus of awareness, the freer you are to experience the *fullness* of your life. The freer you are to fully experience your life, the freer you are to live your life in *wellness*.

As you increase your ability to feel the cycles of life, you create greater stability within yourself by *caring* for your needs in each moment while not being overwhelmed by the highs and lows of being human. As you become more conscious of *life itself*, you're able to consciously create wellness for both yourself and your world through your choices. But, just like strength training at the gym, it requires practice.

PRACTICE

Step 3 of your daily practice starts by you first doing Steps 1 and 2. This pattern of adding to your daily practice, week by week, will continue for the entire program.

Goal

The goal for this week is to relax, come to an "L" position, and feel your cycles.

Breath

Like last week, this week's breathing exercise involves adding a new layer. For each inhalation, as you allow yourself to expand your emotional state from most contracted to least contracted, increase the internal volume of your words.

Start by pairing your most contracted emotional state with a very low internal volume. There's no need for it to be a whisper but rather more like the quietness of a close and intimate conversation. This means that you'll be feeling an emotional state of despair, apathy, boredom, or some other state of being emotionally overcome while quietly affirming that you're healthy.

While expanding your emotional state from most contracted to least contracted, turn up your internal volume to the level that you commonly use when talking with people on the street. This means that you'll be feeling an emotional state of pride, arrogance, self-righteousness, or other feeling that urges you to seek to receive resources while clearly affirming that you are loved.

For each exhalation, as you allow yourself to expand your emotional state from least expanded to most expanded, increase your internal volume even further! This means that you'll be feeling an emotional state of courage, confidence, curiosity, or other state that dissolves blockages to the flow of life as you *assertively* say, "Yes!"

By the time you finish saying "Thank you, Source!", have your internal volume be just short of yelling! This means that you'll be *loudly* feeling an emotional state of gratitude, freedom, oneness, or some other joyous state that increases the flow of life. In other words, you'll be *crying out with joy!*

Then you can lower the volume for the count of each breath as you dial it down in preparation for your next inhalation.

As with last week's practice, this may be challenging for you. So, simply do what you can and observe what happens without losing track of the rest of your breathing exercise. If you find that you can't yet follow all of the instructions, see if you can slow things down a bit, as you would when learning to speak a foreign language.

Movement

After completing Steps 1 and 2 of your daily practice, come to an "L" position on your inhalation by continuing to stand solidly and folding forward to a 90 degree angle at your hips. Be sure that your back is straight and that the crown of your head is pointing straight ahead of you. Extend your head away from your hips, with your shoulders positioned away from your ears and neck. Keep your shoulders aligned with the straightness of your torso as you do this.

Look straight down and bring your arms to match the "L" shape of your body, by having your elbows touch the folded edge of your hips. You can rest your palms on or near your knees to complete the "L".

If you need to press your hands onto your legs to support your back, please do – but only go to 4% past your edge of discomfort. If you're able to hold the position *without* noticeable discomfort to your back, simply hover your palms slightly away from your knees.

As you exhale, slide your hands down the outer sides of your legs as you relax the tension in your back and fold forward even further. This time, allow your head to hang down and see how far you can fold forward without bending your knees, until you reach 4% past your edge of discomfort or can go no further.

In case folding forward doesn't bring you to 4% past your edge, place your hands behind your heels or calves and pull your torso towards your legs until you reach the 4% mark. Be sure to release any tension in your lower back and anus. Feel the difference in your back when you relax it versus when you maintain the tension of the "L" shape.

On your inhalation, use your breath to propel you gently back to the "L" shape, as you slide your hands back up your legs to your knees. As you exhale, slide your hands back down and gently return to your relaxed forward fold for the duration of your out-breath.

AS YOU DID LAST WEEK, LEAD YOUR MOVEMENTS
WITH YOUR BREATH RATHER THAN BREATHING
IN RESPONSE TO YOUR MOVEMENTS.

Continue the cycle for 10 breaths and remember to feel into each cycle fully, along with your sensations and emotions. As you do so, relax the parts of your body that don't require tension to hold your position, noting how your body's requirements change throughout each cycle.

Be sure to do this practice *every day*, for 7 days, before you start Week 4. Also, be sure to go slow, avoiding unnecessary strain.

Be kind and gentle with yourself. It may not seem like you're doing that much physically but the work you're doing in preparing your nervous system is really quite extensive!

Steps

	FOCUS	MOVEMENT	BREATH
1	Feel your sensations	Standing straight	Stage 1
2	Feel your emotions	Forward Folding	Stage 2
3	Feel your cycles	L Position	Stage 3

Beyond

Outside of your daily practice, see how much you can feel your sensations, your emotions, and the cycles of your life in each moment, without reacting to them. If you ever feel distressed at any point throughout your day, simply practice your updated breathing exercise, starting with Stage 1, and remember to "Feel. Love. Now…" – resting assured that the results of your practice are *definitely* worth the effort.

QUESTIONS

Every day, after you do the practice portion of this week's lesson, ask yourself these questions and discover what answers are true for you in the moment.

- Are you allowing yourself to feel grateful as you continue the breathing exercise throughout the practice?

- Are you feeling an urge to skip over, ignore, or otherwise resist following the instructions?

- Are you able to feel your sensations, emotions, and cycles all at once?

- Are you feeling your heartbeat and your blood pumping throughout your body?

- Were you off balance at any point when you were folding forward?

- Have you been maintaining your rate of breathing throughout the practice?

- Are you inspired to feel the cycles of life outside of your practice and, if not, what's in the way of that?

- Did you lose track of the breathing exercise at any point during your practice?

- Did you push yourself *more* than 4% past your edge of discomfort and, if so, why did you choose more discomfort than you needed?

● Are you feeling more stable and at peace than you were before today's practice?

● Are you feeling freer than you were before today's practice and, if not, what's in the way of you feeling freer?

● Have you been feeling your cycles today more than yesterday?

REVIEW

After answering the list of Questions on the *seventh day*, see how much you've mastered this week's lesson by observing whether you've come to realize or understand these key insights:

- ✳ Polarity is what allows for more *and* less.

- ✳ Cycles *oscillate* between more and less.

- ✳ To resist your cycles is to resist the basis of your being *alive*.

- ✳ The *fullness* of your cycles determines the fullness of your life.

- ✳ Light and dark are *not* related to emotions, only to what's visible and what's hidden.

- ✳ Habits lead you to act based on the *past*.

- ✳ Feeling your cycles leads you to act based on the *present*.

- ✳ Habits allow you to conserve your energy by limiting your *awareness*.

- ✳ Awareness is the only way to access *knowledge*.

- ✳ It's by limiting your awareness that you become *unconscious* of the life you're actually living.

- ✳ There is a lot of activity *within you* that you've been unaware of.

- ✳ Living unconsciously *reduces* your ability to function.

- ✳ *Increasing* your consciousness requires devaluing your fears.

✳ As you become *more* conscious of your life, you enable yourself to let go of habits that don't support your wellness.

✳ Becoming more conscious increases your *freedom*.

✳ Increasing your freedom increases your ability to function, which *defines* your wellness.

✳ Resistance to learning is an *inflammatory* response in your body.

✳ What you resist *persists*.

✳ What you condemn, you *maintain*.

✳ Feeling your *hunger* allows you to know when and when not to eat.

✳ Feeling *what* your body is hungry for allows you to know what and what not to eat.

✳ Feeling your body's hunger in each moment allows you to know *how much* to eat.

✳ Feeling your *thirst* allows you to know when and when not to drink.

✳ Feeling *what* your body is thirsty for allows you to know what and what not to drink.

✳ Feeling your body's thirst in each moment allows you to know *how much* to drink.

﹡ Feeling your *tiredness* allows you to know when and when not to rest.

﹡ Feeling how *energized* you are allows you to know when and how much to move.

﹡ The more you feel the cycles of life, the more they inform you what to *attend* to.

﹡ Allow time and space for *relaxing* into the present moment.

﹡ It is up to you to feel *fully* into each moment.

﹡ Expanding your capacity to feel requires *discipline*.

﹡ Coming to *understand* your feelings requires discipline.

﹡ Going *with* cycles gives you energy.

﹡ Going *against* cycles consumes your energy.

﹡ Matter is energy *flowing* in cycles.

﹡ Steadiness in your *breath* brings steadiness to your most basic cycle of life.

﹡ Cycles can *become* bigger or smaller, faster or slower, more even or more erratic.

﹡ Feeling the cycles *outside* of your body allows you to align yourself with them.

﹡ Your breathing exercise helps you to influence and be aware of your *internal* cycles.

* Be kind and *gentle* with yourself.

* Wellness requires *self-care*, not self-sacrifice.

* Relaxation is *key*.

* Relax and *learn* while loving each moment.

Feel Your Self

UNDERSTANDING

In order to truly feel your self, it helps to know what a self truly is. In Week 2, we defined your sense of self as what you use to distinguish what is you from what is not you. But, that only defined your *sense* of self rather than defining what a *self* actually is.

A SELF IS A SET OF PATTERNS USED TO IDENTIFY A LIVING BEING.

Patterns of selfhood allow you to distinguish me from you, us from them, her from him, this community from that community, and more. As a *human* being, your self consists of not only the patterns of your body but also the patterns of your mind. This means that thinking, as in having ideas, about your self is sort of like feeling your feelings.

Since feelings are flows of information within your body, feeling your feelings creates flows of information *about* your body's flows of information. In a similar way, thinking about your self creates mental patterns *about* the mental patterns that you use to identify your self. In other words, thinking about yourself distinguishes what is *you* from what is *not you*, which results in your *sense* of self.

In case this seems confusing to you, just remember that we are physically made of formations of energy, such as atoms. Understanding atoms as forms of energy then allows you to ask yourself, what is it that distinguishes which atoms are part of your body and which ones aren't? After all, you inhale and exhale atoms of air. You drink and urinate, eat and excrete, sweat, fart, cry, and more.

For any given atom, how do you decide whether that atom is part of *you* at any given moment? When do the liquids you last drank and the food you last ate become part of you? Just how far away does an atom need to be from the rest of you to no longer be part of you?

Fundamentally, the only thing that distinguishes whether an atom is or is not part of your self are *the ideas* that you have about yourself. This is because, in reality, everything is interconnected. In reality, we are all just different aspects of one singular unity of existence, distinguishing our selves from other selves in order to have distinct experiences and behaviors.

IT TURNS OUT THAT, BECAUSE TRULY *EVERYTHING* IS INTERCONNECTED, SEPARATION IS ACTUALLY AN ILLUSION OF THE MIND.

What this means is that *you* get to experience being *yourself*, while I get to experience being *myself*. Your neighbor's pets get to experience being *themselves*, while the town you live in gets to experience being *itself*. In every case, each of us is a unique aspect of the unity of our shared existence. That's why it's completely impossible for *us* to truly be separate from *them*. In reality, the only thing that separates "us" from "them" are the thoughts we have, based on illusions that exist solely for the *convenience* of our simple minds.

Like all living beings, the reason you have a self is to maintain it. In other words, the reason you have a set of patterns that identifies your individual existence is to *maintain* your individual existence. If you didn't maintain your individual existence, your body would die and your physical *self* would die along with it.

Our need to survive as individuals is why we evolved to have contractive feelings, to unconsciously *assist us* in maintaining our individual selves. Similar to how we evolved contractive emotions to more easily *maintain* our sense of self, we evolved the mental illusion of separation to more easily *interact* with the complexity of reality beyond the flow of information within our bodies.

Because your self includes mental patterns in the form of ideas, you have a lot of ideas about who you are, what you are, and how you do things. While you're certainly aware of many of those ideas, you're actually *unaware* of a great many more!

SINCE TO FEEL IS TO *BE AWARE* OF THE FLOW OF INFORMATION WITHIN YOUR BODY, TO FEEL YOUR *SELF* IS TO BE AWARE OF THE FLOW OF IDEAS THAT YOU HAVE ABOUT YOURSELF.

Just as you did when you focused on feeling your sensations, emotions, and cycles, this week's lesson is focused on your feeling the flow of ideas you have about yourself *without* reacting to them. This means that you will be feeling whatever ideas arise about yourself *without being attached* to those ideas. In other words, let go of any assumption that the ideas you have about yourself are true!

Still you may wonder, which of your ideas qualify as being about yourself and which ones don't? Certainly if you say to yourself, "I'm a wonderful person", you're expressing an idea about yourself. But, what if you don't actually believe it?

The ideas that define your identity are the ones that you believe. But, here's where things get tricky; you don't need to *believe* that you believe something in order to actually believe it. Instead, you can simply believe something without being aware that you believe it. What's more, you can believe that you believe something when you actually *don't* believe it!

WEEK 4: Feel Your Self

Perhaps you decided at some point that you *should* believe something and so you suppose that you do when in fact you don't.

All of this is to say that the ideas you have about yourself usually *aren't* self-consistent. That's why it's so important to feel the flow of ideas you have about yourself *without* being attached to them.

WHEN YOU'RE ATTACHED TO THE THOUGHTS YOU HAVE ABOUT YOURSELF, MEANING WHEN YOU *BELIEVE* THE THOUGHTS YOU HAVE ABOUT YOURSELF, SUCH ATTACHMENTS CAN EASILY LEAD YOU INTO ENDLESS LOOPS OF THINKING ABOUT YOUR THOUGHTS, WHICH SEVERELY LIMITS YOUR ABILITY TO FUNCTION.

Since illness is a decreased *ability to function*, feeling your self without attachment is *essential* for you to be mentally well and avoid mental illness. That's why it's important for you to be able to discern which of your ideas are about yourself and which ones aren't.

Given that your beliefs about your beliefs may not be accurate, identifying the ideas you use to identify yourself may *seem* difficult but thankfully it's rather easy. All you need to do is determine whether a belief you have is a preference, such as an opinion or a judgement. This means that, if you feel that something is better or worse than something else, you're feeling an aspect of your self. If you feel that something is *neither* better nor worse, such as 2 + 2 being equal to 4, it's not a preference and so isn't part of your sense of self.

Understanding that "better" and "worse" are aspects of our selves allows us to understand that good and bad are never universal. This is because good and bad *only* exist as aspects of selfhood. What *you* may think of as good may be thought of by someone else as bad – and vice versa. That's why *Feel. Love. Now...* doesn't provide instructions on how to be "a good person". Instead, it's about how to create stability and wellness in your life, which is *not* a matter of opinion.

By feeling your self without attachment to your thoughts, you allow yourself to observe your judgements and other preferences without being *entrapped* by them. This means that you avoid getting caught in endless loops of self judgement, which is when your self identifies itself *relative* to itself.

So, who are you, *really*?
And, how does it *feel* to experience your *self*?

Thankfully, you don't need to *try* to be you, because you already are. In fact, you're the *unique and perfect* expression of you.

Whether or not you desire to change yourself, you don't *need* to change in order to be you. So, practice feeling your self by observing your preferences without any need to believe them. Then, as you do, notice how your mental wellness naturally increases.

PRACTICE

Step 4 of your daily practice continues exactly where you left off after completing Step 3, folded forward at your hips.

Goal

The goal for this week is to relax, fold forward with your arms behind your back, and feel your self.

Breath

Like last week, you'll be adding another layer to your breathing exercise. So, be sure to make things easier for yourself by adding each layer of your breathing exercise with each step of your practice, rather than starting Step 1 with Stage 4 of your breathing exercise.

This time, as you inhale, also increase the *intensity* of your emotional state. This is in addition to expressing the meaning of your words internally, increasing the volume of your internal expression, and expanding your emotional state from most contracted to least contracted. This means that, when you're feeling an emotional state of despair, apathy, boredom, or other state of being emotionally overwhelmed, have its intensity be *so faint* as to barely be there.

As you expand your emotional state from most contracted to least contracted, turn up the intensity of your emotions to the level that you most commonly experience in your day-to-day life. This means that you'll be feeling an emotional state of pride, arrogance, self-righteousness, or other feeling that urges you to seek to receive resources at a level of intensity that you find to be rather normal.

As you exhale, increase the intensity of your emotional state even further. While you allow yourself to feel an emotional state of courage, confidence, curiosity, or other state that dissolves blockages to the flow of life, start to raise the intensity *beyond* your normal range of emotional experience.

By the time you finish saying "Thank you, Source!", have your emotional intensity be as strong as you can manage! This means that you'll be *intensely* feeling an emotional state of gratitude, freedom, oneness, or some other joyful state that increases the flow of life. In addition, you'll probably find yourself smiling unintentionally! You can then lower your emotional intensity for the count of each breath in preparation for your next inhalation.

Movement

Continuing on from Step 3, folded forward at your hips, bring your arms behind your back. As much as you're able to, clasp your hands together firmly, almost as if you're forming the shape of a pistol. This means that your thumbs and index fingers will be pressed together in an "L" shape while the rest of your fingers interweave to create a firm grip.

On your inhalation, straighten your knees while folding forward, with a relaxed head and back. Extend your arms with your index fingers pointed straight up to the sky, as far away from your back as you can without going more than 4% past your edge of discomfort. If you can't point your fingers straight up, just get them as close as you can without going more than 4% past your edge.

You will likely need to squeeze your shoulders together behind your back to extend your arms further away from you. But, this can easily become straining. So, be gentle with yourself and relax the parts of your body that aren't required to maintain the position.

On your exhalation, bend forward even further and bring the front of your shoulders as close as possible to touching your knees. This will likely require you to bend your knees — but bend them only as much as you need in order to get as close as you can to touching your knees with your shoulders. Keep your arms outstretched away from your back but *tilt your arms forward* so that your index fingers point more in the direction of your head than straight up.

Be sure to move slowly and go no more than 4% past your edge of discomfort. Also, remember to do the breathing exercise for a count of 10 breaths and to breathe deeply, regardless of any awkwardness or discomfort you may feel. Focus on feeling your self, your sensations, your emotions, and your cycles.

This practice may stir up a lot for you. So, be kind. If you feel any harsh judgements, forgive both yourself and others to help you release the emotional and physical tension associated with them. The less tension you create and the more you allow yourself in each moment to be who you *are* rather than who you *think* you should be, the greater the stability and wellness you create for yourself.

FEEL. LOVE. NOW...

To help you relax and be gentle with yourself, this week's practice also includes an *optional* step for you.

After completing this week's *prescribed* practice, remain folded forward and release your hands from behind your back. Let your arms hang in front of you with your hands touching opposite elbows, just like you've been doing for Step 2.

Relax your back completely and just hang there. Continue your full breathing exercise for 10 more breaths and simply feel your body release any extra tension that you may still have in your head, neck, shoulders, and back.

If you find that the optional step doesn't feel good to you, don't do it. It *is* optional, after all. If you find that it *does* feel good, though, please practice the step even though it's optional. If you find that it doesn't feel good *today*, you may just find that it starts to feel good when you try it again tomorrow. In either case, be sure to do this week's practice *every day* for 7 days before you start Week 5.

Steps

	FOCUS	MOVEMENT	BREATH
1	Feel your sensations	Standing straight	Stage 1
2	Feel your emotions	Forward Folding	Stage 2
3	Feel your cycles	L Position	Stage 3
4	Feel your self	Arms behind & fold	Stage 4

Beyond

If you don't already own a yoga mat, I recommend that you buy one this week. You'll likely appreciate having it ready for next week's practice. Be sure that any yoga mat you purchase isn't slippery and isn't stretchy but *is* easy for you to grip. The weeks to come will reference positions for your hands and feet that are relative to the mat.

Outside of your daily practice, see how much you can feel your sensations, emotions, cycles, and self in each moment, without reacting to them. If you feel distressed for any reason, simply practice your updated breathing exercise and remember to "Feel. Love. Now..." – knowing that you've already made substantial progress!

QUESTIONS

Every day, after you do the practice portion of this week's lesson, ask yourself these questions and discover what answers are true for you in the moment.

- Are you allowing yourself to be grateful that you get to be you and, if not, what's in the way of that?

- Are you allowing yourself to feel any irritation that comes up without reacting to it?

- Are you able to feel your sensations, emotions, cycles, and self all at once?

- How limited are you by self preservation?

- Are you being completely honest with yourself about what you're really feeling?

- Did you lose your balance at any point during the practice, even slightly?

- Are you able to maintain all of the layers of the breathing exercise at the same time?

- Are you inspired to feel your self outside of your practice and, if not, what's in the way of that?

- Did you push yourself *more* than 4% past your edge of discomfort and, if so, why did you choose more discomfort than you needed?

- Are you feeling more stable and at peace with your self than you were before today's practice?

- Are you feeling freer than you were before today's practice and, if not, what's in the way of you feeling freer?

- Have you been feeling your self today more than yesterday?

REVIEW

After answering the list of questions on the *seventh day*, see how much you've mastered this week's lesson by observing whether you've come to realize or understand these key insights:

* A self is a set of patterns used to *identify* a living being.

* Patterns of selfhood identify what you *experience* as being either you or not you.

* Your self consists of *mental* patterns as well as physical ones.

* Thinking about yourself results in your *sense* of self.

* Whether an atom is or is not part of your self is determined by *the ideas* you have.

* In reality, everything is *interconnected.*

* Separation is simply an illusion of the *mind.*

* Each of us is a unique aspect of the *unity* of our shared existence.

* What differentiates "us" and "them" are merely *ideas.*

* You are *never* truly alone.

* Thank you for being *you.*

* You have a self in order to *maintain* your individual existence.

* Your body constantly engages in *threat assessment* to maintain itself.

✳ Your body requires *reassurance* to feel safe.

✳ Withdrawing into your self *decreases* your influence on the world.

✳ We evolved to have contractive feelings in order to *survive* as individuals.

✳ We evolved to have expansive feelings in order to *thrive* collectively.

✳ Contractive emotional stories are self *maintenance* programs.

✳ Contractive emotions subconsciously *express* your sense of self.

✳ Expansive emotions are felt *beyond* your self.

✳ To *feel* your self is to be aware of the flow of ideas that you have about yourself.

✳ The ideas that you have about yourself *need not* be true.

✳ The ideas that define your identity are the preferences that you *believe.*

✳ You can believe something without *believing* that you believe it.

✳ The ideas you have about yourself are often *inconsistent.*

✳ Endlessly thinking about your thoughts severely *limits* your ability to function.

✳ Conjecture can be used to *empower* fear.

✳ Self *acceptance* is required for your wellness.

＊ Feeling your self without attachment is *essential* for you to be mentally well.

＊ Your preferences, opinions, and judgments are *always* part of your sense of self.

＊ Self judgement is when your self identifies itself *relative* to itself.

＊ There is no need to use your experiences to *justify* judging your self.

＊ "Good" and "bad" only exist as aspects of *selfhood*.

＊ Your stability and wellness are *objective*.

＊ Without even trying, you are the unique and *perfect* expression of you.

＊ Who you were is not who you *are* and also not who you will be.

＊ Who you will become depends on your *choices*.

＊ *Accept* your self, both as you are and as you were.

＊ There's discomfort in the *difference* between who you are and who you believe yourself to be.

＊ The less tightly you hold onto your sense of self, the *easier* it is to be you.

＊ Nothing *outside* your sense of self can save you from what you feel *inside* your sense of self.

＊ Threats to your sense of self are easily *misidentified* as threats to your survival.

✳ As pain signals a threat of harm, it can be *painful* to alter your sense of self.

✳ It harms you to *internalize* external conflicts.

✳ It harms *others* to externalize internal conflicts.

✳ Feel and *release* your resistance to change.

✳ Expanding your capacity to feel requires *discipline*.

✳ Coming to *understand* your feelings requires discipline.

✳ Relaxation is *key*.

✳ Relax and *learn* while loving each moment.

Feel Your Relationships

UNDERSTANDING

In the not-so-distant past, human relationships were more commonly referred to as social bonds, a term that implied attachment and adhesiveness. In comparison, the word "relationships" is about *relating*, which refers to connecting two or more things without any sense of longevity.

From your experiences of being in relationship with other human beings, you've probably noticed that human relationships are more substantial than a simple connection would be. After all, since separation is an illusion, you're actually in connection with *all of existence* either directly or indirectly. So, what *are* relationships?

FUNDAMENTALLY, RELATIONSHIPS ARE *ASSEMBLIES* OF
THOUGHTS, FEELINGS, AND ACTIONS
THAT *INTERCONNECT* ONE OR MORE LIVING BEINGS.

In the same way that a self is used to identify a living being, a relationship is used to identify what *connects* one or more living beings. However, while both selves and relationships are useful in identifying things, they have very different *purposes.* While the purpose of your self is to maintain your self, the purpose of your relationships is to *facilitate your growth.*

Of course, just because relationships facilitate your growth that's not to say they're always supportive! In fact, relationships can also be *extractive,* whenever resources are being drained through the relationship. In each moment, your relationships can range anywhere from completely supportive to completely extractive. Yet, how you choose to *grow* in relation to your relationships is always up to you.

As a human being, your growth is facilitated by *both* the support of being nurtured *and* the support of being challenged to grow beyond your comfort zone. Certainly it's not as though someone needs to be your cheerleader in order for you to have a relationship with them! Instead, each of your relationships offers a unique blend of thoughts, feelings, and actions that change over time, continuously offering you new ways to grow.

Seeing as this week's lesson is about *feeling* your relationships, it's important to understand that feeling your relationships is *not* the same as how you feel *about* your relationships. How you feel *about* a relationship is how you feel your *sense of self* in relation to that relationship. This means that how much you like or dislike a given relationship is based on how you *identify yourself* at a given time relative to that relationship.

When you *feel your relationships,* what you're doing is feeling *into* the thoughts, feelings, and actions that constitute those relationships.

For example, what do you think of when you think about a person you're in relationship with? How do you feel when you're with that person? How do you behave with that person? How does that person behave with you?

Because relationships evolve over time, it's helpful for you to treat them as living beings *themselves.* For instance, you can imagine them as vines that bridge the gaps between trees of individuality. In a sense, you can seed and plant relationships, nurture them, stress them, and even kill them. However, it's not entirely up to you how your relationships are conceived, grow, diminish, or die. Certainly, the environment of your relationship and the living beings you're in relationship with each have their own influence on how your relationships evolve.

As you feel more deeply into your relationships, you might notice that they seem to have a will of their own.

There is no need to *manipulate* your relationships, in the same way that there is no need for your relationships to manipulate *you.* Instead, feel your relationships by witnessing and honoring them. Remember, they exist in order to facilitate your growth. So, what do they need in order to grow in *wellness*? Is there something you can give them to increase *their* ability to function?

When relationships between two living beings are supportive, they help to increase the ability of *both* beings to function. This means that supportive relationships create *wellness.*

When relationships are *extractive*, however, they decrease the ability of *one or both* living beings to function. This is how extractive relationships create *illness*. Understanding this quality of relationships is what allows you to create wellness *through* your relationships, by ensuring that your relationships are as supportive as possible rather than extractive.

Whether or not you've previously recognized it, you are always in relationship with yourself. So, how might you nurture that relationship to be more supportive?

In addition to your relationship with your self, there are many *categories* of relationships, such as familial, friendly, adversarial, romantic, professional, communal, and societal. Each category of human relationship you have defines a *range* of possible thoughts, feelings, and actions. If you wish, you can think of relationship categories as similar to species of trees, expressing common patterns of growth while still allowing each tree to be unique.

This week, similar to what you've done in prior weeks, feel your relationships without reacting or emotionally attaching to them. Remember, relationships are *living* assemblies of thoughts, feelings, and actions that interconnect one or more living beings. So, witness them, honor them, and care for them as you would a rose bush in your garden.

Feeling your relationships may feel wonderful, awful, or anywhere in between – and that's perfectly fine! Simply focus on feeling them as they are, remembering that they exist to facilitate your growth in all of their beauty and complexity.

PRACTICE

Step 5 of your daily practice continues where you left off with Step 4, folded forward at your hips. Starting this week, however, you will be referencing positions on your yoga mat.

You can think of your yoga mat as being like a runway for airplanes. The portion of the runway that airplanes first fly over as they come in to land corresponds to the *base* of your yoga mat. In comparison, the last portion of the runway that airplanes fly over as they take off corresponds to the *top* of your yoga mat.

Much of the time, you will be aligned with your yoga mat in the same way that an airplane is aligned for takeoff or landing. However, there will also be times when you'll be facing *perpendicular* to your mat, towards the left or the right. When that's the case, you will be positioned *lengthwise* relative to your mat.

Goal

The goal for this week is to relax, have your hands and feet on your mat, and feel your relationships.

Breath

As with last week, you'll be adding another layer to your breathing exercise. With each inhalation, as you allow yourself to expand your emotional state from most contracted to least contracted, imagine a small, jet-black, marble-sized sphere sitting at the bottom of the inside of your stomach. As you inhale, imagine the sphere getting bigger and brighter. By the end of your inhalation, allow for the sphere to have grown large enough to surround your body and bright enough that you no longer imagine it having any darkness at all.

With each exhalation, as you allow yourself to expand your emotional state further from least expanded to most expanded, imagine that the sphere of light surrounding you grows even larger and brighter as you exhale. By the end of your exhalation, allow for the sphere to have grown large enough to surround the entire Earth and bright enough to match the intensity of the Sun.

As you practice expanding the imaginary sphere from your quietest and most emotionally contracted state to your loudest and most emotionally expansive state, you may notice that the sphere expands in different ways when you're inhaling as compared with when you're exhaling.

Because the bottom of the inside of your stomach is roughly the center-point of your body, when the marble-sized sphere expands to encompass you on your inhalation the sphere is quite literally centered on you! In contrast, when the sphere of light expands on your exhalation it mostly expands *downwards,* as it encompasses and becomes centered on the Earth. It's as if you were blowing up a giant balloon of light beneath your feet.

IN THIS WAY, YOUR BREATHING EXERCISE ACTS
AS A REMINDER FOR YOU
TO *GRATEFULLY ACKNOWLEDGE* THAT,
THOUGH YOU ARE A PART OF THE WORLD,
THE WORLD IS NOT CENTERED ON YOU.

Movement

To begin Step 5 of your movement exercise, stand at the base of your yoga mat and come to an "L" position, similar to the one you did for Step 3. However, this time stretch your arms out ahead of you towards the top of your mat, in alignment with your back. From this position, tilt your torso down, extend your hands, and come into an angled position with your hands and heels securely on the mat.

You may recognize the position you're in as a yoga pose commonly referred to as "downward-facing dog". However, you can let go of any notions you may have regarding the "right way" to be in the pose. Instead, just focus on following these instructions and feel into your practice.

Place your hands on the mat with your arms extended straight. If you're able to do so, put half of your body weight on your hands. It may feel almost like you're holding the floor up above your head.

Keep your back straight and align your arms with your back. This will form one branch of the angle that, combined with your mat, will then form a triangle when viewed from the side. Of course, depending on your flexibility, you may not be able to keep your legs straight and form a truly triangular shape with your torso. However, that's not the objective here.

Instead, focus on keeping your butt as high in the air as you can while keeping your arms and back straight, with your heels on the ground.

You can bend your knees as much as you need to in order to maintain the pose.

Starting with your legs in a comfortable position relative to your torso, slowly extend your feet back towards the base of your yoga mat until you feel that you're 4% past your edge of discomfort. From this position, start to perform your updated breathing exercise, maintaining the pose for 10 deep breaths.

Relax any part of your body that isn't required to maintain the pose, including your neck. This means that your head will be hanging down without any effort needed to hold it up. As you relax into the pose, you may notice your body becoming more comfortable with it. So, feel free to adjust the positions of your hands and legs slightly in order to stay just 4% past your edge of discomfort.

You may notice that being in the pose stretches your calves and hamstrings. This is especially common if you spend a lot of time sitting on seats every day, which has unfortunately become commonplace despite being a physically unhealthy behavior. So, this week's practice includes an optional step for you to loosen the tension in your legs.

Coming out from your pose, keep your left foot at the base of your yoga mat and extend your right leg towards the top of your mat. This will bring you towards a pose commonly referred to as "the splits".

While keeping your right leg straight with your heel on the mat, bend your left leg as much as needed until your left knee is touching the mat. If you need to hold yourself up using your hands, please do!

Adjust the position of your left knee so that you're just 4% beyond your edge of discomfort, while keeping your back and head straight. If you start to become more comfortable in the position, you can bend forward slightly at your waist to stay at 4% past your edge.

While continuing your updated breathing exercise, hold the pose for a count of 10 breaths. Then, switch your pose so that your left leg extends forward to the top of your mat while your right knee is resting on the mat. As you continue your breathing exercise, hold this new pose for another 10 breaths and feel how the tension in your legs and thighs lessens throughout the week.

Steps

	FOCUS	MOVEMENT	BREATH
1	Feel your sensations	Standing straight	Stage 1
2	Feel your emotions	Forward Folding	Stage 2
3	Feel your cycles	L Position	Stage 3
4	Feel your self	Arms behind & fold	Stage 4
5	Feel your relationships	Downward dog & splits	Stage 5

Beyond

Since we as human beings evolved to stand on our feet and walk around, it helps the wellness of our bodies to do so. So, starting this week, you are highly encouraged to walk for a total of at least 30 minutes throughout your day. As you do, take the opportunity to feel into your sensations, emotions, cycles, self, and relationships.

Feel into the cyclical movement of your legs, feet, and hips as you walk. Release any attachments you may have to the stories you use to define yourself and instead feel into the fullness of your life as it is in each moment.

Remember to do your practice *every day*, for 7 days, before starting Week 6. If you start to feel bored or otherwise distressed at any point during your day, simply practice your breathing exercise starting from Stage 1 and discover how it feels to be in relationship with your world, remembering to "Feel. Love. Now..."

QUESTIONS

Every day, after you do the practice portion of this week's lesson, ask yourself these questions and discover what answers are true for you in the moment.

- How is your relationship with yourself today?

- Which of your relationships are strongly supporting your growth at this time?

- Are you able to feel your sensations, emotions, cycles, self, and relationships, all at once?

- Did you avoid going all the way to 4% past your edge of discomfort?

- Are you able to maintain all the layers of your breathing exercise at the same time?

- Are you grateful for the relationships you currently have?

- Are you nurturing the growth of your relationships?

- Are you being honest with yourself and others about what you're really feeling?

- Did you push yourself *more* than 4% past your edge of discomfort and, if so, why did you choose more discomfort than you needed?

- Are you feeling more stable and at peace than you were before today's practice?

- Are you feeling freer than you were before today's practice and, if not, what's in the way of you feeling freer?

- Have you been feeling your relationships today more than yesterday?

REVIEW

After answering the list of questions on the *seventh day*, see how much you've mastered this week's lesson by observing whether you've come to realize or understand these key insights:

* Human relationships *identify* human connections.

* Relationships are assemblies of thoughts, feelings, and actions that *interconnect* living beings.

* The purpose of your relationships is to facilitate your *growth*.

* Your relationship with yourself *also* exists to facilitate your growth.

* Supportive relationships *increase* the ability of those in relationship to function.

* Extractive relationships *decrease* the ability of those in relationship to function.

* Your growth is supported *both* by being nurtured and by facing challenges.

* You grow when you *learn* from your relationships.

* Your relationships consist of thoughts, feelings, and actions that *evolve* over time.

* To feel your relationships is to feel into the thoughts, feelings, and actions that *constitute* those relationships.

* Expanding your capacity to feel requires *discipline*.

FEEL. LOVE. NOW...

✳ Coming to *understand* your feelings requires discipline.

✳ Understanding is structural but mostly *nonverbal.*

✳ There are many *categories* of relationship available for you to have.

✳ Each category of relationship defines a *range* of possible thoughts, feelings, and actions.

✳ Relationships can *shift* from one category to another.

✳ Relationships are *alive* and have a will of their own.

✳ In each moment, your relationships can be any degree of *well or ill.*

✳ In each moment, your relationships can be any degree of *stable or unstable.*

✳ In each moment, your relationships can be any degree of *supportive or extractive.*

✳ Living in and expressing *gratitude* increases the desire of others to *support* you.

✳ Feeling your relationships involves *witnessing, honoring,* and *caring* for them.

✳ The action of caring is *powerful.*

✳ You learn *how* to care for things by relating.

✳ As your relationships facilitate your growth, you have *no need* to manipulate them.

∗ As *living beings*, relationships are able to be conceived, grow, diminish, and die.

∗ Both directly or indirectly, you are in relationship with the entire *world*.

∗ The world is *not* centered on you.

∗ Each person is a *unique* expression of humanity.

∗ As you are in relationship with *others*, you are also in relationship with *yourself*.

∗ Your relationship with yourself influences your growth *more* than any other relationship.

∗ For others to *trust* you, you must first trust yourself.

∗ The behaviors you are most troubled by in others are ones you *deny* in yourself.

∗ You cannot experience what you *disallow* others to experience from you.

∗ In relationship, you have to be *yourself* to be recognized.

∗ Your authenticity is more *valuable* than your inauthenticity.

∗ As you appreciate others being in service to you, be in service to *others*.

∗ Nurture your relationships by *supporting* their growth with ease.

∗ Allow being in relationship to be *easy*.

FEEL. LOVE. NOW...

✳ Wise people are *relaxed*.

✳ Relaxation is *key*.

✳ Relax and *learn* while loving each moment.

Feel Your World

UNDERSTANDING

No matter how small it may seem at times, the world we share is wonderfully large. No matter how much and how far you travel, you will never be able to visit all of it. There will always be some city, town, or village that you didn't have time to see. There will always be some stretch of water you didn't have time to sail across and some island that you didn't have time to dock at. Even if you have time to return and revisit a place, it will be a different experience than the one you had on your prior visit.

In comparison, the individual worlds we live in are wonderfully small. Just compare the number of relationships you'll ever have with the number of grains of sand on a single beach. Compare how many relationships you'll ever have with the number of jobs you'll ever have, compared with the number of people you'll ever marry.

The world that you are able to feel in each moment is truly tiny. Yet, it's also vastly detailed! Can you feel how *rich* your world truly is? Can you feel its complexity of color, shape, size, and texture? Can you feel its sounds, smells, touches, and tastes?

Notice how the more *alive* your world is – the richer it feels. Notice how the more alive your world is – the more it *changes*. Notice how the more it changes and the richer it is the more there is for you to feel.

AS YOU'VE COME TO FULLY FEEL YOUR SENSATIONS, EMOTIONS, CYCLES, SELF, AND RELATIONSHIPS, YOU'RE NOW READY TO FEEL THE *REST* OF YOUR WORLD.

Feel the water and the land, the animals and the people, the buildings, the infrastructure, and the vegetation. Feel how they all come together to form your world. Feel how your world is far *grander* than any stories you could ever have about it. Feel how you are a part of your world and how your world is an extension of you.

Because feelings are a flow of information within your body, feeling your world starts within you. Even though your physical senses receive plenty of external stimulation, most of what you perceive to be your external world is actually *internal* to your individual experience. This is why *how* you choose to perceive has a tremendous influence on *what* you perceive, regardless of how your senses are stimulated.

To fully feel your world, you need to be *open* to it. The more closed down and contracted you feel, the less information there is available to you about the world you're truly living in. The less information there is available to you about your world, the more you are feeling stories of selfhood in place of the *riches* of your world.

FEELING YOUR WORLD IS A NEVER-ENDING PROCESS OF DISCOVERY, INVOLVING EXPANSIVE FEELINGS OF COURAGE, CONFIDENCE, CURIOSITY, CARING, ACCEPTANCE, PLAYFULNESS, GRATITUDE, FREEDOM, AND ONENESS.

As you were reminded by last week's breathing exercise, the world we share is not actually centered on you. In fact, you and I are the equivalent of bacteria on the skin of our mother Earth. However, as human beings we have an outsized influence on our world.

Similar to how the cells in your body work together to form organs and your organs work together to allow your body to function, we as human beings behave like cells in the bodies of larger organisms. We form groups, and groups of groups, combining our knowledge, skills, and labor to achieve things in the world far beyond what any of us can do as individuals.

WHEN YOU FEEL YOUR *WORLD*, WHAT YOU'RE FEELING IS THE *BEAUTY* OF THE SYNERGY AND COOPERATION OF A WHOLE THAT'S *FAR GREATER* THAN THE SUM OF ITS PARTS.

Like every community, every tree, and every drop of water, we each have our roles to play on the world stage. No matter how you're acting, you're always in service to something, even if only to yourself. So, as you feel your world, feel how you fit into it. Feel how you're being in service and what you're being in service to.

Feel how you are a part of your family, your business, your community, and your society. Feel how you are a part of the air, water, land, and fire that make up life on Earth. As separation is an illusion, the life that you feel in the world beyond your sense of self is *your* life. This world that you're feeling is *your* world. So, feel what is being created and what is being destroyed. Feel how much life is being nurtured and how much life is being consumed.

Feel your world – because it is only when you do so *fully* that you can fully love.

PRACTICE

As you may have noticed, your practice is designed to build in complexity each week. This means that it's also extending in length, which makes it progressively easier to be interrupted. So, while it's best that you complete your daily practice without stopping, if you *are* interrupted in your practice it's helpful to know how to recover from an interruption.

For example, if you are interrupted in the middle of Step 4 of your practice, it's best to restart Step 4 from a count of 1. Yet, you may find it difficult to maintain all 4 layers of your breathing exercise while recovering smoothly from an interruption. So instead, begin with Step 1 for a count of one breath, then Step 2 for one breath, and so on until you've included all of the layers you need to restart a count of 10 breaths for the Step that was interrupted.

As your practice increases in duration, you may find that you appreciate having music playing in the background. If you do, be sure that the music is not jarring or distracting and that the tempo of the music is rather slow. Keeping your music slow and soothing is useful to avoid losing your focus and to avoid speeding up your breathing.

Also, as you transition between the steps in your practice, you are welcome to use transitions as opportunities to express what's true for you in your body. This means that you are welcome to express yourself as pliable or assertive, feminine or masculine, flowing, sharp, chaotic, lyrical, or subtle. Really any variation you desire to express with your body is welcome as you dance the dance of life. After all, this is *your* daily practice, for *your* body, heart, mind, and spirit.

For Step 6 of your daily practice, you'll be transitioning to stand up straight again. And, you'll also be adding one last layer to your breathing exercise.

Goal

The goal for this week is to relax, roll your head around on your shoulders, and feel your world.

Breath

For this week's breathing exercise, as you imagine an expanding sphere centered on yourself with each inhalation, also imagine that you're breathing in love from the world. Imagine that the love you're breathing in is what is filling the sphere, making it bigger and brighter.

With each exhalation, as you imagine the sphere of light that surrounds you growing to surround the Earth, also imagine that you're breathing love out into the world. Imagine that the love you're breathing out is what is causing the sphere to glow as brightly as the Sun and expand at the speed of light, surrounding and filling the planet with love.

As you practice breathing love in, notice how it fills you and empowers you. As you practice breathing love out, notice how it grows and rapidly expands in its influence. In this way, you'll be getting ready for Section II.

Movement

To begin Step 6 of your daily practice, position yourself roughly in the middle of your yoga mat and stand on it *lengthwise*. Stand up *straight,* as you learned for Step 1, and raise your arms to form a "T" shape as you begin your updated breathing exercise.

Slowly and gently, bring your left ear toward your left shoulder and softly roll your head around on your shoulders clockwise. Do your breathing exercise for a count of 10 breaths before switching directions to roll your head around on your shoulders counter-clockwise for another 10 breaths.

Be *very* careful, by relaxing your neck and going very slowly. In this case, be sure to go only to the *edge* of discomfort in your neck and not past it. There's no need for your breathing to be aligned with the movement of your head here, either. So, take your time and feel where in your body you can relax while still maintaining a stable stance.

The focus of this step of your practice is to keep your arms and shoulders stable as you roll your head around safely. The best way to do this is to extend your arms *outward* to maintain a "T" shape while keeping your shoulders down. If you find that you can't hold your arms up in this way for the entire time, keep your arms extended outward with your shoulders down as you gradually reduce the angle of your arms only as much as you need in order to maintain the stability of your stance.

If you feel tension in your neck, let go of any thoughts of the future. You may find that your breathing exercise helps you to direct your focus away from any discomfort in your arms. You may also find it especially helpful in this case to feel the movement of your belly as you breathe.

AS IT'S IMPORTANT THAT YOU NOT PINCH YOUR VERTEBRAE
WHEN TILTING YOUR HEAD BACK,
AVOID FORCING YOUR NECK TO STRETCH
AND INSTEAD FOCUS ON *RELAXING* YOUR NECK MUSCLES.

Steps

	FOCUS	MOVEMENT	BREATH
1	Feel your sensations	Standing straight	Stage 1
2	Feel your emotions	Forward Folding	Stage 2
3	Feel your cycles	L Position	Stage 3
4	Feel your self	Arms behind & fold	Stage 4
5	Feel your relationships	Downward dog & splits	Stage 5
6	Feel your world	Head rolling	Stage 6

Beyond

If you ever find the world spinning around you, whether inside or outside of your daily practice, remember that you're able to create stability within yourself no matter how unstable it may seem. Simply "Feel. Love. Now..."

Feel your sensations, emotions, cycles, self, relationships, and world *without* being reactive to them. Love yourself and others, your relationships, your communities, your society, and your world. Be *present* with your world and you will experience the stability that is always available within you.

Remember to do your daily practice *every day*, for 7 days, before reading the Section I Review. And, if you ever feel distressed, just practice your breathing exercise starting at Stage 1 and discover how much wellness and stability you've *already created* within yourself.

QUESTIONS

Every day, after you do the practice portion of this week's lesson, ask yourself these questions and discover what answers are true for you in the moment.

- How does your world feel to you in this moment?

- How do you fit into your world?

- What is your sense of purpose in life?

- Are you able to feel your sensations, emotions, cycles, self, relationships, and world all at once?

- Did you feel overwhelmed at any point during the practice?

- How does it feel to *not* be the center of your world?

- Were you able to maintain all of the layers of your breathing exercise at the same time?

- Do you feel grateful for your world as it is, regardless of what you may prefer to be different?

- Are you feeling more stable and at peace than you were before today's practice?

- Are you feeling freer than you were before today's practice and, if not, what's in the way of you feeling freer?

- Have you been feeling your world today more than yesterday?

REVIEW

After answering the list of questions on the *seventh day*, see how much you've mastered this week's lesson by observing whether you've come to realize or understand these key insights:

✳ Your world is *vast*.

✳ Your *encounter* with your world is small.

✳ Your *experience* of your world is detailed.

✳ Your world is very much *alive*.

✳ You live *with* your world, not just *on* it.

✳ You are *part* of your world.

✳ Your world is an *extension* of you.

✳ When *you* are unbalanced it may appear that your world is unbalanced.

✳ Most of what you *perceive* as your external world is actually internal.

✳ *How* you perceive has a tremendous influence on *what* you perceive.

✳ To fully feel your world, you need to be *open* to it.

✳ Expanding your capacity to feel requires *discipline*.

✳ Coming to *understand* your feelings requires discipline.

✳ The more *contracted* you feel, the less information you receive about your world.

✳ Feeling your world is a never-ending process of *discovery*.

✳ Human beings are like *bacteria* on the skin of our mother Earth.

✳ The *influence* of human beings on our world is tremendous.

✳ We form groups to achieve things *far beyond* what any of us can do as individuals.

✳ To feel your world is to feel the beauty of *synergy*.

✳ Cooperation is what allows the *whole* to be far greater than the sum of its parts.

✳ *Real* problems reduce the ability of the whole to function.

✳ We *each* have our roles to play in this world.

✳ Wherever you are is where you're supposed to *be*.

✳ You are always in service to *something*, even if only to yourself.

✳ Feel *how* you're being in service and *what* you're being in service to.

✳ Feel what is being *created* and what is being *destroyed*.

✳ Feeling your world *fully* allows you to fully *love*.

✳ Your world is what gives you a sense of *purpose*.

✳ A life of purpose is more *valuable* than a life of success.

✳ Allow yourself to be *grateful* for your world.

✳ Your world is constantly *changing*.

✳ Accept your world as it *is* in each moment.

✳ Improve your world by *loving* your world.

✳ *Allow* your world to heal.

✳ Relaxation is *key*.

✳ Relax and *learn* while loving each moment.

Feel
It All

Congratulations on completing Section I!

IF YOU'VE FINISHED ALL OF THE WEEKLY LESSONS SO FAR, YOU'VE COME A *LONG* WAY IN LEARNING HOW TO FEEL!

To see just how far you've come, please take some time to revisit what you've learned by re-reading the review sections for Week 1 through Week 6. As you'll likely gain new insights, it's definitely worth the trouble!

Because people often learn more effectively by doing than by reading or listening, much of what you are meant to learn from *Feel. Love. Now...* is actually a result of you *incorporating* its lessons into your daily life. So, once you've re-read the review sections for Week 1 through Week 6, see how much you've mastered the material for Section I by discovering whether you've come to realize or understand *these* key insights:

✳ Feelings *differentiate* physical, mental, emotional, and spiritual well-being.

✳ The relaxing of your body, mind, heart, and spirit are *intertwined*.

✳ Relaxing is the most important thing you can *do*.

✳ Relaxing is *essential* for you to feel fully.

✳ You must *allow* yourself to feel in order to feel fully.

✳ *Welcoming* your feelings allows them to be in service to your growth.

✳ Feelings flow *within* you; life flows *through* you and *around* you.

✳ Living requires *being* alive, not *doing* a life.

✳ Doing cannot *fix* your being.

✳ You live to *thrive*, not just to survive.

✳ Gratitude for living requires an *openness* to life.

✳ It's more useful to go *with* the cycles of life than against them.

✳ It's more useful to *welcome* polarity than to neutralize it.

✳ Comfort and discomfort are *not the same* as pleasure and displeasure.

✳ Discomfort is *required* to live a fulfilling life.

✳ Relaxing in the midst of discomfort *frees you* to be well.

✳ Increasing your ability to function is what *makes* you well.

✳ Decreasing your ability to function is what makes you *ill*.

✳ Illness is its *own* punishment.

✳ To heal is to gain *wellness*, by increasing your ability to function.

✳ Being well requires you to be *aware*.

✳ Internal stability requires *self-awareness*.

✳ Breathing slowly, deeply, and *evenly* helps you to relax your nervous system.

✳ You can *lead* your life with your breath.

✳ You *create* your emotional state through the stories you choose.

✳ You must open your *self* to learn and grow.

✳ Release all fear of being *you*.

✳ Growing can be *uncomfortable* but is essential for your wellness.

✳ To be well you must be *free* to change yourself.

✳ You needn't *try* to be yourself, because you already are.

✳ Resisting what's true for you *denies* your freedom to be you.

✳ Your individuality is your *uniqueness* of expression.

✳ To be truly free is to be free of *resistance*.

FEEL. LOVE. NOW...

✳ Resistance is when a flow loops *inward* instead of continuing onward.

✳ You must have peace *inside* yourself to have peace *outside* yourself.

✳ Without love it can be challenging to hold the *tension* of peace.

✳ All is one; you *are not* separate.

✳ Your wellness and the wellness of others are *interrelated*.

✳ It's more important to *be* here than to go somewhere.

✳ Achievement is merely *icing* on the cake of life.

Now... are you ready for Love?

Section II
LOVE.

Love Life

UNDERSTANDING

To understand how to *love* life, you'll first need to understand what life actually is. After all, life is *everywhere* on Earth. So, for you to understand what life is is sort of like a fish understanding what an ocean is – and, just as a fish is part of the ocean, you are a part of life on Earth. This means that your understanding of what it means to be alive is sort of like a fish understanding what it means to be wet.

FUNDAMENTALLY, LIFE IS A PROCESS WHICH BOTH *CREATES* ITSELF AND *CONSUMES* ITSELF.

In fact, pretty much all of the food you've ever eaten was alive at some point. This feeding of life on itself is necessary because energy can only be *repurposed* rather than created or destroyed. As the energy from the Sun and Earth available for life is *limited* over time and space, life must consume itself in order to grow more fully and freely.

The continuous creation and consumption of life, that is life itself, produces a sort of boiling stew of being. You might even imagine it as a pot of boiling water, resulting in bubbles forming, changing shape, and bursting. Every person, plant, and animal, bacterium, fungus, and microorganism is part of life's bubbling into being.

Every living being changes form through conception, growth, diminishment, and death, just as bubbles do. And, because separation is an illusion, all of the *magnificence* that is life is an extension of you, just as you are an aspect of *it*.

Clearly, such a glorious thing as life is worthy of being loved! But, why does life *exist*?

LIFE EXISTS TO EXPERIENCE *BEING*.
THIS IS *WHY* YOU HAVE FEELINGS
AND ALSO WHY YOU DO THINGS.

The flow of information that allows feelings to exist allows living beings to react and respond, increasing the variety of what's possible to experience by increasing the complexity of possible interactions. This is why – the more fully you're *feeling,* the more fully alive you're *being*. It's also why – whatever you're *doing* is merely a *consequence* of your being. But then, what is *love*?

As a term, "love" is quite possibly the most overused word in the English language, a way to express affection, enthusiasm, adoration, romance, sexuality, popularity, and more. But here, "love" refers simply to a specific knowing and desire one feels, as well as a specific thing one does.

LOVE IS A KNOWING AND DESIRE TO *INCREASE THE ABILITY TO FUNCTION* OF WHATEVER IS BEING LOVED, WHILE "TO LOVE" IS TO *ACT IN SUPPORT* OF THAT KNOWING AND DESIRE.

In other words, you *feel love* for something when you feel a knowing and desire to support its wellness – and you *love* something when you act in support of the love you feel for it. This is why this program is titled "Feel. Love. Now..." rather than "Love. Now, Feel."

When you allow yourself to *feel* love, you open and expand the state of your nervous system to engage more fully with life. When you're *in* love, you're in that expanded state, in relation to whatever you're in love *with*. So, when you *love life,* you're truly in love with life!

When you allow yourself to *follow* love, you allow love to *guide* your actions. This is why love is *central* to the guidance system you are assembling for yourself using these instructions. It's also why contractive emotions, which exist to maintain your sense of self, are *never loving*. Rather, love leads you *beyond* your sense of self, beyond all of your fears, your wants, and your pride, while also guiding you to *love yourself*.

As you may have noticed, feeling love can involve feeling attraction *towards* something. But, feeling love can also involve feeling attraction *away* from something else. For example, you may feel attracted to doing certain things out of love that attract you away from making money, attempting to increase your status, or valuing your thoughts and expectations.

As love inherently supports wellness, love *heals*. And, because wellness is an increased ability to function, you can never be a slave to love. Rather, love *sets you free*, free from the "shoulds" and "supposed-tos", free to be you, and free to be fully alive!

When you *don't* act in support of the love that you feel, you deny and refuse to follow your built-in guidance system towards wellness. This is why a life filled with love is a life of wellness while a life *without* love is a life of illness.

When you *love life*, you are acting on your desire to support the wellness of the unfolding of creation. You are embracing and cherishing the *magnificence* of all creation by feeling how you may be in support of its wellness and by choosing to act on those feelings in each moment. No matter the circumstances, *life* is worth loving.

PRACTICE

Goal

The goal for this week is to relax, extend your torso, and love life.

Breath

Rather than adding another layer to your breathing exercise, this week you'll be *removing* layers from your breathing exercise. Specifically, you'll be removing layers 2, 3 and 4. This means that you'll be continuing to say the words to yourself ("I am healthy. I am wealthy." and so on) while breathing deeply and evenly, with your lips open and your tongue pressed lightly to the roof of your mouth.

You will also continue imagining an expanding sphere of light being inflated by receiving love on your inhalation and giving love on your exhalation. But this time, on your inhalation, allow the expanding sphere of light to be centered on your heart and continuously filled with swirling colors. On your exhalation, instead of expanding the sphere to envelope the Earth, expand the sphere of swirling colors from your heart and let it keep expanding *infinitely* outwards into the Universe, like ripples in a still pond.

Instead of contracting and expanding your emotional state during your breathing exercise, have your emotional state be as *expansive* as you can manage. Instead of lowering and raising your internal volume and intensity, have your internal volume and intensity be set as *loud and high* as you can. This means that you will be saying the words to yourself at a consistently high internal volume while allowing yourself to consistently feel *intense* joy!

THIS VERSION OF YOUR BREATHING EXERCISE
ALLOWS YOU TO FOCUS ON *FEELING AND EXPRESSING* LOVE.

Movement

Step 7 of your movement exercise continues close to where you left off with Step 6, standing up straight. For this next step, though, spread your feet a little further so that the distance between your feet is the same as the distance between your shoulders. The easiest way to do this is by moving your right foot further to the right so that the inside of your foot is now where the outside of your foot *was* when you were standing straight. Then, move your left foot to the left in the same way.

As you begin your updated breathing exercise, bring your hands as far above your head as possible, pressing your palms together. Then, while keeping your hips stable and your upper body straight, slowly angle your upper body in a clockwise spiral and extend your torso. This means that your fingertips will be "drawing a spiral" as you slowly angle your upper body further away from your center, as if your upper body was a spinning top beginning to wobble.

Once you've reached 4% past your edge of discomfort in extending your torso (perhaps immediately) turn your spiral into an ellipse and continue the movement clockwise for a count of 10 breaths. Have the movement be *very slow* while keeping your breaths slow, deep, and even.

There's no need to synchronize the timing of the ellipses with your breathing. Instead, focus on extending your hands as far as possible from your waist so as to stretch your upper body throughout the *entire* step. In order to keep your upper body straight, be sure to keep your head centered between your arms as you move and avoid tilting your chin up.

Once you've angled your upper body in a clockwise ellipse for 10 breaths, switch directions and continue for another 10 breaths. Remember to maintain your updated breathing exercise for both directions and be sure to do your practice *every day*, for 7 days, before starting Week 8.

Steps

	FOCUS	MOVEMENT	BREATH
1	Feel your sensations	Standing straight	Stage 1
2	Feel your emotions	Forward Folding	Stage 2
3	Feel your cycles	L Position	Stage 3
4	Feel your self	Arms behind & fold	Stage 4
5	Feel your relationships	Downward dog & splits	Stage 5
6	Feel your world	Head rolling	Stage 6
7	Love life	Torso extending	Loving

Beyond

Outside of your practice, begin to consciously *feel love* by expanding your emotional state. If you ever have any difficulty, simply practice your full breathing exercise, starting with Stage 1. It will quickly remind you how to consciously expand your emotional state to feel love.

Remember, "Feel. Love. Now..." is a memory aid to know what to do in each moment. So first, *feel fully*. Then, *love life*, acting upon the love that you feel in each moment. As you do so in each moment, you'll be supporting the wellness of all life, life that you're so *very* blessed to be part of!

QUESTIONS

Every day, after you do the practice portion of this week's lesson, ask yourself these questions and discover what answers are true for you in the moment.

- How does it feel to be alive?

- How does love feel to you?

- Do you feel love guiding you in each moment?

- Are you able to feel love while also feeling your sensations, emotions, cycles, self, relationships, and world all at once?

- Are you grateful to be alive?

- Are you feeling more stable and at peace than you were before today's practice?

- Are you feeling freer than you were before today's practice and, if not, what's in the way of you feeling freer?

- Were you able to maintain the layers of the breathing exercise for each step of your practice?

- How does it feel to transition during your practice from cycling through your emotions to fully embracing love with each breath?

- Did you start to get off balance during your practice?

- Did you maintain the stability of your hips?

- Are you in love with life?

REVIEW

After answering the list of questions on the *seventh day*, see how much you've mastered this week's lesson by observing whether you've come to realize or understand these key insights:

* ✳ You are part of the *magnificence* that is life on Earth.

* ✳ Life is a process which both *creates* itself and *consumes* itself.

* ✳ Living to *consume* consumes your own life.

* ✳ Energy can only be *repurposed* rather than created or destroyed.

* ✳ Limited energy requires life to consume itself to *grow* more fully and freely.

* ✳ Living beings *change form* through conception, growth, diminishment, and death.

* ✳ Life exists to experience *being.*

* ✳ You have feelings and do things to experience *being.*

* ✳ Whatever you do is a *consequence* of your being.

* ✳ The flow of *life* is the infinite, feminine flow of information in transformation.

* ✳ Life and love are about what you put *into* them, not what you get out of them.

* ✳ Be *intimate* with life.

* Life is *its own* reward.

* Life is meant to be *lived*.

* Living is an *art*.

* Love is a *knowing and desire* to support the wellness of whatever is being loved.

* *Thinking* is not knowing.

* Thinking is a form of *dreaming*.

* Thinking frees you from being *stuck* when not in your knowing.

* Keep calm and carry on with *love*.

* You love whenever you *act* in support of the love you feel.

* You feel love by *opening and expanding* the state of your nervous system.

* Being fully well requires engaging fully with an *open heart*.

* You're *in love* with whatever your nervous system relaxes open to welcome in.

* Expanding your capacity to love requires *discipline*.

* Truly *understanding* love requires discipline.

* When you allow yourself to *follow* love, you allow love to *guide* your actions.

* Love leads you *beyond* your sense of self.

FEEL. LOVE. NOW...

✳ Contractive feelings, which exist to maintain your sense of self, are *never* loving.

✳ Love *cannot* truly harm you.

✳ Love isn't always *fun.*

✳ Love isn't always *comfortable.*

✳ Love sets you *free.*

✳ Love *heals.*

✳ *Live* from Love.

✳ A life filled with love is a life of *wellness.*

✳ A life without love is a life of *illness.*

✳ You *love life* when you act on your desire to support the wellness of life itself.

✳ Resisting your love for life is *futile.*

✳ Relaxation is *key.*

✳ Relax and learn while *loving* each moment.

Love Yourself

UNDERSTANDING

In order to truly love life, it's essential that you love *your* life. This means that, though each of us may be a tiny piece within the magnificent tapestry of life itself, loving life requires you to *love yourself*. However, loving yourself is not the same as loving your *sense of self*.

Since your self is a set of patterns used to identify you as a living being, it turns out that you are actually *more* than your self. More than any patterns or ideas you have about yourself, you are an aspect of life itself – which means that you are *alive* and able to function both fully and freely. It is this *ability to function* that allows you to be well, to be ill, to be loved, and to love.

TO LOVE YOURSELF IS TO *ACT* UPON THE KNOWING AND DESIRE TO INCREASE YOUR OWN ABILITY TO FUNCTION.

The reason it was so important for you to learn to fully feel your sensations, emotions, cycles, self, relationships, and world before learning to fully love yourself is that you can only love yourself as you *are* in each moment, not as you *think* you are or should be. To love yourself you must *accept* yourself as you are, similar to how you would love a small child regardless of how they behave.

Loving yourself, loving who you are in each moment, is *essential* to creating wellness and stability not only in your life but also in the lives of others. Loving yourself is not only *not selfish*, it's actually *required* for you to be able to love life beyond yourself.

TO BE *SELFISH* IS TO ACT
FROM CONTRACTIVE EMOTIONAL STATES,
SUCH AS *FEAR, WANT, AND PRIDE,*
RATHER THAN ACTING FROM
EXPANSIVE EMOTIONAL STATES OF LOVE.

In all its forms, fear is a *virus*. And like all viruses, fear commands its host to behave in ways that further the *spread* of the virus rather than supporting the wellness of the host. Fear does this by triggering a type of inflammation in your nervous system, resulting in feelings of resistance that make it more difficult to feel and think freely. This is why it is most empowering to feel your fears *fully* while ignoring their commands.

To be in fear is to judge life as a threat, seeking to maintain your *ideas* at the cost of what is actually *present*. To be in want is to be in lack, seeking to get whatever it is you *think* you need, regardless of what it is that you *actually* need. To be in pride is to be in *want* of others to affirm that you're "good enough" to be loved, seeking to appease your *fears* of being judged as insufficient. In comparison, *loving yourself* attracts you to what you *truly* need in order to increase your ability to function as an aspect of life itself.

FOR YOU TO BE SELFLESS IS FOR YOU TO SERVE OTHERS WHILE *NEGLECTING* TO LOVE YOURSELF.

This is why selflessness creates illness and why loving yourself *never* involves being selfless – nor being selfish. Instead, to love yourself simply requires *you* to love you. So, *love* being you! Enjoy the *feeling* of being you. Enjoy the *experience* of being you. After all, no one but you gets to be you!

You are *unique*, a special and precious living being who gets to both love and be loved. *Appreciate* that you have a sense of self that allows you to distinguish between what is you and what is not you. Of course, *believing* what you think about yourself is *not* the same as appreciating your sense of self.

In fact, love *isn't* affected by what you think about yourself! As you learned in Week 4, you define your sense of self through your preferences, opinions, and judgments. Yet, to love is to act upon the knowing and desire to increase the ability of things to function, *regardless* of anyone's preferences.

You make your preferences, opinions, and judgments in order to *define* yourself, not to love yourself. Yet, no matter how much your preferences change, you are still you. This means that your preferences, opinions, and judgments in any given moment *are never true* outside of the fact that you *believe them* in that moment.

Having preferences, opinions, and judgments helps you to think *for* yourself and *about* yourself. So, it's helpful for you to understand that the reason you think is to solve problems, which can only exist *relative* to your sense of self. Life, however, is *not* a problem to be solved. This is why loving yourself *does not* require you to think.

During the evolution of our species, our human minds became increasingly clever, which allowed us to solve ever more complex problems. As a result of this, your mind is rather like an exceptionally strong hammer that treats everything and anything as a nail, which can result in a lot of damage.

It's important for you to know when and *when not* to use the hammer of your mind. And, it turns out that love provides the answer. Because to love is to act upon the knowing and desire to increase the ability of things to function, your mind is best used to determine *how* to act upon love's desire when you *aren't* feeling love's knowing. Of course, this requires you to solve problems that you may not *know* how to solve, which is why curiosity is an expansive and loving emotion.

When you *think* you know everything that you need to know in order to solve a problem, you think you're in control. And yet, there are always things that you don't know that you don't know, which means that – in reality you're *never* in control!

LIKE THE IDEA OF SEPARATION,
CONTROL IS AN ILLUSION OF THE MIND
TO MAKE IT EASIER TO SOLVE PROBLEMS BY *ASSUMING*
THAT YOU KNOW ENOUGH TO TRULY SOLVE THEM.

The illusion of control provides you with an illusion of safety, because it assumes that you know enough to handle whatever threats come your way. However, because you never know whether or not you know enough, it's more useful to *release* control and instead rely on love.

Because separation is an illusion, love is not just *for* you or just *from* you. In fact, love is everywhere and *in* everything! The plants and animals you encounter are often living in love, increasing the ability of life to function. And, now is a great time for you to do so as well, starting with yourself.

When you allow yourself to feel love and act upon the love you feel, you are letting go of not only control but also resistance. To trust love is to trust life and to trust *your* love is to trust that your life is growing towards ever-increasing wellness. When you instead choose to *resist* love, to resist your feelings of love or resist acting upon those feelings, you are resisting the stability and wellness of your own growth.

SO, ALLOW LIFE TO FLOW
BY ALLOWING *LOVE* TO FLOW,
STARTING WITH YOURSELF.

As you love yourself, you increase your ability to function – which increases your ability to love, creating a virtuous cycle of upliftment for all. Truly, it is a blessing to *all* for you to love yourself. You see, as love sets you free, resistance to love is indeed futile.

PRACTICE

Goal

The goal for this week is to relax, revolve your hips, and love yourself.

Breath

For this week's portion of your breathing exercise, continue to breathe love as you did in last week's portion.

Movement

Step 8 of your daily practice continues where you left off with Step 7, standing up with your feet shoulders-width apart. For Step 8, spread your feet a little further apart by moving your right foot further to the right so that the inside of your foot is now where the outside of your foot *was* in Step 7. Then, move your left foot to the left in the same way.

As you continue your breathing exercise from Step 7, place your hands above your hips (but below your ribs) while slowly extending your hips to the left. Then, begin to revolve your hips clockwise around the center point between your feet.

If you visualize slowly stirring a pot of soup by having the stirring spoon sweep the inner edge of the pot while the handle of the spoon remains straight, your upper body will be equivalent to the handle – with your hips equivalent to the *tasty* part of the spoon.

As you slowly revolve your hips clockwise, extend no more than 4% past your edge of discomfort. If you're not able to reach 4% past your edge, spread your feet further apart until you *are* able. Relax the parts of your body that are not required for the movement, such as your anus. Let go of any need to align your breathing with the pace of your movement.

RELEASE ANY RESISTANCE YOU ENCOUNTER,
ANY SENSE OF "SHOULD" OR "SHOULDN'T",
CHOOSING TO RELAX INTO YOUR PRACTICE
AND TRUST IN LOVE.

After revolving your hips for a count of 10 deep breaths, continue your breathing exercise and switch the direction of your hips. Continue for another count of 10 breaths, making sure to love yourself and to love life.

Steps

	FOCUS	MOVEMENT	BREATH
1	Feel your sensations	Standing straight	Stage 1
2	Feel your emotions	Forward Folding	Stage 2
3	Feel your cycles	L Position	Stage 3
4	Feel your self	Arms behind & fold	Stage 4
5	Feel your relationships	Downward dog & splits	Stage 5
6	Feel your world	Head rolling	Stage 6
7	Love life	Torso extending	Loving
8	Love yourself	Hip revolving	Loving

Beyond

Be sure to do your practice *every day*, for 7 days, before starting Week 9. Outside of your daily practice, continue to focus on *loving yourself* by feeling the love you have for you – and acting on it. If loving yourself feels odd to you, imagine loving someone whom you adore and check to see that you're making similar choices for yourself as you would make for the person you adore.

If you ever have any difficulty, remember to "Feel. Love. Now..." All it takes to start is to *feel fully*. Then, love your life by *loving yourself* in the present moment. As you do, you'll be supporting not only the stability and wellness of *your* life but of *all* life.

QUESTIONS

Every day, after you do the practice portion of this week's lesson, ask yourself these questions and discover what answers are true for you in the moment.

- How does it feel to love yourself?

- Do you feel the difference between love and fear?

- Do you feel the difference between love and want?

- Do you feel the difference between love and pride?

- Do you believe that you are worthy of love?

- Do you agree with yourself?

- Are you grateful to be you?

- Are you resisting loving yourself fully?

- Are you resisting doing your daily practice?

- Are you feeling more stable and at peace than you were before today's practice?

- Are you feeling freer than you were before today's practice and, if not, what's in the way of you feeling freer?

- How did it feel not to change the breathing exercise for this step?

- Did you enjoy yourself?

- Are you in love with yourself?

Review

After answering the list of questions on the *seventh day*, see how much you've mastered this week's lesson by observing whether you've come to realize or understand these key insights:

* ✳ To truly love life, you must love *your* life.

* ✳ Loving life requires loving *yourself.*

* ✳ Loving yourself is not the same as loving your *sense* of self.

* ✳ As a part of life, you are *more* than the patterns that define your self.

* ✳ Your ability to *function* allows you to be well, to be ill, to be loved, and to love.

* ✳ To love yourself is to *act* upon the knowing and desire to increase your wellness.

* ✳ *Welcome* self love.

* ✳ You *cannot* fight your self and win.

* ✳ Be in *service* to love, starting with yourself.

* ✳ You can only love yourself as you *are* in each moment.

* ✳ You cannot love yourself as you *think* you are or should be.

* ✳ To love yourself, you must *accept* yourself as you are.

* ✳ Loving yourself requires healing by way of *forgiveness.*

* ✳ Loving yourself is *not* selfish.

✳ Loving yourself is *essential* to creating wellness and stability in the lives of others.

✳ To be *selfish* is to act from contractive emotional states, such as fear, want, and pride.

✳ Fear is a *virus*.

✳ Viruses are instructions that proliferate by altering the way their hosts *behave*.

✳ Viruses affect behaviors by dictating *illness* in their hosts.

✳ Fear facilitates resistance by causing inflammation in your *nervous system*.

✳ Resistance to feeling and thinking *decreases* your ability to function.

✳ To be in fear is to judge life as a *threat*.

✳ To be in want is to be in lack of what you *think* you need.

✳ To be in pride is to be in want of others to affirm that you're *good enough* to be loved.

✳ Maintaining peace and equanimity within yourself is an *antiviral* practice.

✳ From the perspective of fear, peace is *delusional*.

✳ Release *all* fear of love.

✳ It is not the presence of fear but rather *believing it* that is harmful.

✳ In place of believing in *fears,* believe in the glory of *love.*

✳ Love isn't troubled by what you *think* about yourself.

✳ Your preferences, opinions, and judgments exist to *define* yourself, not to love yourself.

✳ Your preferences, opinions, and judgments are *never true* beyond your believing them in any given moment.

✳ Having preferences, opinions, and judgments helps you to think *for* yourself and *about* yourself.

✳ To be selfless is for you to serve others while *neglecting* to love yourself.

✳ Loving yourself does *not* require you to think.

✳ You think in order to solve *problems* relative to your sense of self.

✳ Life is *not* a problem to be solved.

✳ When mistaking life as a *problem* to be solved, the only solution is death.

✳ Your mind is best used to determine *how* to act on love's desire when you can't feel love's knowing.

✳ When you think you know what you *need* to know to solve a problem, you think you're in control.

✳ In reality, you're *never* in control.

✳ Control is an *illusion of the mind.*

✳ The only way to even *try* to control life is to end it.

✳ The illusion of control provides you with an illusion of *safety*.

✳ It's more useful to *release* control and instead rely on love.

✳ Expanding your capacity to love requires *discipline*.

✳ Truly *understanding* love requires discipline.

✳ Love is not just *for* you or *from* you; it's everywhere and in everything.

✳ To trust in love is to trust in *life*.

✳ You are *worthy* of love.

✳ Self love supports you in *being* you.

✳ When you *resist* love, you resist the stability and wellness of your own growth.

✳ Resisting your love for yourself is *futile*.

✳ Relaxation is *key*.

✳ Relax and learn while *loving* each moment.

Love the Contrasts

UNDERSTANDING

You've probably noticed that love *isn't* always easy, especially if you've had a child or a challenging intimate relationship. Your desire to increase the ability of those you love to function can easily come in conflict with contractive feelings such as fear, want, and pride, whether in yourself or others, resulting in pain and emotional discomfort. This is why it's important for you to embrace the *contrast* between the highs and lows of love.

Since love is a knowing and desire for wellness in what you love, it may appear at times that there are right ways and wrong ways to love. Yet, that's *not* truly the case. This is because acting on the love you feel *isn't* about right and wrong, which are tied to your sense of self. Instead, loving is about how you're *increasing* the ability of what you love to function – and how you may be *decreasing* that ability to function as a consequence of the choices you make. So really, love is *beyond* your sense of self.

As love is the desire for wellness, there's *nothing* conditional about it. If you stop feeling your love for someone when they do something you don't like, it's not that the love *itself* went away; it's because you stopped *feeling* the love by contracting your nervous system to prevent or reduce the intensity of emotional pain. This means that what was conditional was not your love but rather your *loving*, in how you chose to *act* on the unconditional love that is always accessible to you. See the contrast?

Loving through both the highs and the lows is *essential* for you to create stability and wellness in your life. This is because your desire to increase the ability of things to function doesn't stop when doing so becomes *inconvenient* for you. This is why love is about *accepting*, rather than *excepting*. It's why love is *inclusive*, rather than *exclusive*. See the contrasts?

As you open yourself to witness the unconditional, inclusive desire of the love in your heart to increase the wellness of life, *appreciate* its contrasts.

Love it *all*, through the highs and the lows, the pleasure and the pain, the wellness and the illness, and beyond. Love *beyond* your discomfort, *beyond* your hesitation, and *beyond* your edge – not too far – but just far enough to grow and expand your ability to love it all, through it all.

As love can attract you to things, it's helpful for you to know that attraction is a result of polarity, which you learned about in Week 3. It turns out that the attraction of opposites is what *powers* the cycles of life. In fact, the attraction between the masculine and feminine aspects of life has powered the evolution of life on Earth for over *a billion* years! So, please, love the contrasts of life while *also* understanding that it's the contrasts of life that *empower* love.

If you've heard of the notion that "like attracts like", it can be confusing to learn that attraction is a result of *opposition*. On the other hand it's rather obvious that, in order for both sides to exist, left needs right and right needs left. Up needs down and down needs up. Light needs dark and dark needs light. So, rather than referring to the attraction of opposites, what is meant by the phrase "like attracts like" is *resonance*.

Resonance is the reinforcing of cycles by other cycles. It's what makes an acoustic guitar sound much louder than an unamplified, non-acoustic guitar. It's what makes pendulums swing together and people join with like-minded individuals.

You can understand resonance simply as how the universe makes things *more similar* over time. Rather than being in conflict with the attraction of opposites, resonance is actually *necessary* for it. After all, if left is attracted to right and right is attracted to left, what's keeping the left on the left and the right on the right *in spite of* their attraction? Clearly, the left is resonating with the left while the right is resonating with the right. So really, it's quite alright!

What all this means is that you are living, along with everyone and everything else, in *energetic fields* of resonance and opposition. These fields flow and shift, stabilize and destabilize, creating the unending flowering of forms that is life. So, let go of any fears you may have about the changes or differences that you experience in your life and, instead, *love the contrasts*.

Welcome with love whatever resonates with you. Welcome with love whatever opposes you! Love it all, through it all, in spite of it all, and because of it all.

Choose to love by choosing to cooperate with *both* those you resonate with *and* those you oppose. Choose cooperation in place of conflict by *operating with* rather than *fighting with* others. This doesn't mean you need to agree, resonate, or go along with others against your will. Cooperating with others means operating *with* them; it doesn't mean that you need to follow their orders. You can instead let others resonate *with you* rather than you choosing to resonate with them.

COOPERATION IS ESSENTIAL
BECAUSE YOU CAN ONLY LOVE YOUR LIFE
WHEN YOU *TRULY* LOVE THE CONTRASTS OF LIFE ITSELF.

Because contrasts are what empower the force of love, by loving the contrasts you're actually loving *love*. The more you love the contrasts, the stronger the force of love becomes, the stronger it affects you, and the more powerfully love guides you. This is how you increase the *power* of your internal guidance system to create a life of wellness and stability.

PRACTICE

Goal

The goal for this week is to relax, rotate your torso, and love the contrasts.

Breath

For this week's portion of your breathing exercise, continue to breathe love as you did in last week's portion.

Movement

Step 9 of your daily practice continues where you left off with Step 8, standing with your feet wider than shoulders-width apart. Let your arms fall gently to your sides as you continue your breathing exercise unchanged. In fact, you will be maintaining your breathing exercise unchanged for *all* of the steps in Section II.

Keeping your upper body straight and upright, with your feet pointed straight ahead, turn your hips to the left and allow your upper body, head, and arms to follow without *any* extra effort. Once you've turned as far to the left as you can using only your hips, turn your hips to the right and do the same thing, alternating directions to allow your body to turn back and forth.

Gently increase the speed of your rotations, with your knees and legs maintaining a stable stance, until you're just 4% past your edge of discomfort. This will likely cause your arms to swing around your body, resulting in them slapping at your sides. Be sure to go slow at first and avoid overextending your arms or slapping your torso too hard.

AS YOU MIGHT DISCOVER YOUR ARMS SWINGING FURTHER THAN YOU THOUGHT, TAKE CARE TO AVOID INJURING YOURSELF AND OTHERS!

While continuing your breathing exercise, alternate the rotation of your upper body in both directions for a count of 10 deep breaths. As you do so, you'll notice that the twisting action of your upper body constricts your breathing somewhat. So, make sure to breathe deeply and *love the contrasts* between breathing with ease and breathing with difficulty as well as the contrast between left and right.

Steps

	FOCUS	MOVEMENT	BREATH
1	Feel your sensations	Standing straight	Stage 1
2	Feel your emotions	Forward Folding	Stage 2
3	Feel your cycles	L Position	Stage 3
4	Feel your self	Arms behind & fold	Stage 4
5	Feel your relationships	Downward dog & splits	Stage 5
6	Feel your world	Head rolling	Stage 6
7	Love life	Torso extending	Loving
8	Love yourself	Hip revolving	Loving
9	Love the contrasts	Torso rotating	Loving

Beyond

Be sure to do your practice *every day*, for 7 days, before starting Week 10. Outside of your practice, remember to *love the contrasts* by feeling the polarities and resonance of life while loving it all! If you ever have any difficulty, simply practice your breathing exercise and remember to "Feel. Love. Now..."

As you learn to feel and love the contrasts, you'll discover that doing so helps you to be *present* enough and *empowered* enough to create a life of wellness and stability, no matter how high or low things go.

QUESTIONS

Every day, after you do the practice portion of this week's lesson, ask yourself these questions and discover what answers are true for you in the moment.

- How does it feel to love the contrasts?

- Are you able to love in the midst of pain and discomfort?

- Did you try to control how your upper body rotated during the practice?

- Are you resisting loving amidst the lows of your life?

- Are you hesitant to love amidst the highs of your life?

- Are you being fully inclusive with your love?

- How easy is it for you to forgive when you truly love the contrasts?

- Are you feeling more stable and at peace than you were before today's practice?

- Are you feeling freer than you were before today's practice and, if not, what's in the way of you feeling freer?

- Did you start to get off balance during the practice?

- Did you lose track of your breathing exercise during the practice?

- Are you scared of loving the contrasts?

- Are you in love with the contrasts?

REVIEW

After answering the list of questions on the *seventh day*, see how much you've mastered this week's lesson by observing whether you've come to realize or understand these key insights:

* Love *isn't* always easy.

* Contractive feelings can be in *conflict* with the love you feel, resulting in pain and discomfort.

* Acting on the love you feel *isn't* about right and wrong.

* Loving is about supporting the wellness of what you love through your *choices*.

* There's *nothing* conditional about love.

* Your loving can only be conditional in how you *choose* to act on love.

* Fear of *being judged* is a fear of conditional love.

* Loving through *both* the highs and the lows is essential to creating stability and wellness in your life.

* Your *desire* to love doesn't stop when loving becomes inconvenient.

* Love is about *accepting*, rather than *excepting*.

* Love is *inclusive*, rather than *exclusive*.

* Appreciate the *contrasts* of love.

✳ Love it *all*, through the pleasure, the pain, and beyond.

✳ The *only* thing in the way of love is pain and fear.

✳ Pain signals a *threat* of harm.

✳ Pleasure signals a fulfillment of *desire*.

✳ Pleasure is the *aliveness* you feel.

✳ Pleasure is *required* for you to truly live.

✳ Love is required for you to truly *thrive*.

✳ Expanding your capacity to love requires *discipline*.

✳ Truly *understanding* love requires discipline.

✳ To grow and expand your capacity to love, love a little bit *beyond* your edge.

✳ How *fully* you love reveals how fully well you are.

✳ Fill yourself with love to rise *above* the pain.

✳ Whoever isn't filling their hearts with love is missing out on *bliss*.

✳ Attraction is a result of *polarity*.

✳ The attraction of opposites is what *powers* the cycles of life.

✳ The *contrast* of opposites is what empowers love.

✳ The seeming attraction of *similar* things is resonance.

✳ Resonance is the reinforcing of *cycles* by other cycles.

✳ Resonance allows things to become more similar over time *without* opposition.

✳ You live in *energetic fields* of resonance and opposition that allow life to flow.

✳ Love supports the contrasts of life in order to enable *growth*.

✳ Welcome with love whatever *resonates* with you.

✳ Welcome with love whatever *opposes* you.

✳ Cooperate with both those you resonate with *and* those you oppose.

✳ Disagreement is *inevitable* but conflict is not.

✳ Choose cooperation in place of conflict by *operating with* rather than *fighting with* others.

✳ Loving the contrasts empowers *love itself*.

✳ You increase the *power* of your internal guidance system by loving the contrasts.

✳ By loving the contrasts you become a human expression of love *loving love*.

✳ Resisting the power of love is *futile*.

✳ Relaxation is *key*.

✳ Relax and learn while *loving* each moment.

Love Beauty

UNDERSTANDING

Let's face it; love is *beautiful* – and the more love you feel, the more beautiful it is! Have you noticed that, when you're in love, colors look somehow richer, sounds seem somehow more detailed, and food somehow tastes better?

When you open yourself to fully feel love, you naturally get to feel the beauty of what *is*. You get to experience the joy of *accepting* the world as it is in the present moment, regardless of how *or* how much you'd like to change it.

If you find the beauty of love to be difficult to relate to, consider what it might mean for you to love your own child. Yes, you may prefer that they stop banging the table with the cutlery or stop kicking the chair. You may lovingly tell them to stop what they're doing and be more considerate of others. Yet, your love for them still allows you to experience the joy of *accepting them* as they are in each moment. You see, in the eyes of a loving parent, a child is *always* beautiful.

Beauty is the combination of an entity's aspects that you feel as *pleasurable.*

So, beauty is always "in the eye of the beholder". This is because what pleases you is only what you *allow yourself* to be pleased by. As a result, the more you accept your world as it is, the more beautiful your life becomes!

Yet, as love is a knowing and desire to create wellness – it may appear at times that love is about being *displeased* and changing what is, such that love and beauty are at odds with each other. It may then surprise you to know that love and beauty are *strongly* linked.

This is because we *love* what we consider beautiful and consider *beautiful* what we love.

Since you feel *both* beauty and love, your body knows of the connection between them *instinctively.* This is why advertisers and marketers have made use of your body's innate attraction to love so as to *subconsciously* attract you towards buying products and services. This is done *not only* when advertising makes use of beautiful models, actors, scenes, and images. Have you noticed that, in high quality advertising, the colors look somehow richer, the sounds seem somehow more detailed, and the food looks absolutely delicious?

Advertising, marketing, entertainment, and product development have often attempted to reduce pain and heighten the pleasurable *stimulation* of beauty so as to trick your body into believing that you're *in love*. Your *attraction* towards higher fidelity sound in music and higher quality video on more immersive screens is related to this same instinct.

The confusion in your body between love and beauty, which your body associates with reduced pain and heightened levels of pleasure, is a basis for addiction. Because love is the basis of life itself, the *strong desire* that you feel when you're deeply in love is the strongest force of attraction possible in your life. This is why being in love with your *real* life frees you from addiction. It's why opening yourself to feel *real* love, instead of relying on artificially beautiful substitutes, is *essential* for you to create wellness and stability in your life.

Still, the link between love and beauty is not one to be broken but rather one to be blessed! As a conscious human being, you are entirely able to influence both yourself and others *subconsciously*, the same way that advertisers, marketers, and other influencers do. This means that, by *creating* beauty while loving life, you can actively use the power of affecting the subconscious to create wellness.

A LIFE FILLED WITH LOVE IS A *BEAUTIFUL* LIFE
AND A LIFE FILLED WITH BEAUTY IS A LIFE TO BE *LOVED*.

Perhaps you've noticed that, whether in art, design, ornamentation, or otherwise, people *deeply enjoy* creating and sharing in beauty. This deep enjoyment essentially acts as an invitation to love, an invitation to share in a desire for the freedom, oneness, and gratitude of wellness. It is this *subconscious* invitation to love that encourages people to express their femininity by adorning themselves with makeup, jewelry, fine clothing, and accessories.

As femininity is receptive, responsive, and reactive while masculinity is penetrating, directed, and steady, it is your femininity which is *attractive* and your masculinity which is *attracted*. This means that it is your masculinity which desires to *witness* beauty and your femininity which desires to *be beautiful*. It is your masculinity which *desires* to love and your femininity which desires to *be loved*. It is your femininity which feels the beauty and love of *form* and your masculinity which feels the beauty and love of *function*.

TO LOVE BEAUTY IS TO INCREASE
THE *ABILITY* OF THINGS TO BE PLEASURABLE.

As beauty is strongly linked with love, it's important to understand that beauty *is not* linked with perfection. Rather, perfection is simply the matching of a result with an *idea* of what the result "should be". As beauty is the combination of a thing's aspects that you feel as pleasurable, perfection can only be seen as beautiful when it pleases you to have your expectations met.

When you're in love with life *as it is,* you are able to see the beauty of things no matter how perfect *or* imperfect those things may be. So clearly, beauty is not perfection and perfection is not beauty. In fact, perfection *itself* can be deemed imperfect – just as imperfection can be deemed perfect as it is.

TO LOVE THE BEAUTY OF *LIFE* IS TO LOVE THE BEAUTY OF WHAT IS.

So, love the beauty of love loving life. Love the beauty of love loving beauty. Love beauty in your life and let the pleasure of beauty support you in living a *beautiful* life. Truly, life *is* beautiful, just as it is.

PRACTICE

Goal

The goal for this week is to relax, have one hand down as low as you can with your other hand up as high as you can, and love beauty.

Breath

For this week's portion of your breathing exercise, continue to breathe love as you did in last week's portion.

Movement

Step 10 of your movement exercise continues where you left off with Step 9, standing with your feet wider than shoulders-width apart. However, with Step 10 you'll be starting to switch things up a bit. As you may have noticed, Steps 5 through 9 didn't require you to synchronize your breath with your movements. Starting with Step 10, though, you'll be synchronizing your breathing with your movements once more. So, remember to lead your movements *with* your breath rather than leading your breath with your movements.

On your inhalation, as you stand solidly with your feet facing forward, extend your arms outwards in the shape of a "T". With your palms facing forward, have your fingers and thumbs extended to form "L" shapes with your hands.

On your first exhalation, bend forward at your waist and turn your upper torso to your left. Once you've done so, place your right hand on your mat in front of your left foot. Have your four extended fingers pointing *perpendicular* to your foot, with your extended thumb almost touching your big toe. This will form a sort of "L" shape between your left foot and your right hand.

If you aren't flexible enough yet to form the "L" shape with your hand and foot, simply adjust as needed so that you are *no more than* 4% past your edge of discomfort. This may require you to grasp your foot, shin, or knee with your hand instead of placing it on your mat.

Keep your arms extended during *both* your inhalation and exhalation, as though there was a long pole connecting your left wrist with your right wrist the entire time. This means that your left hand will be raised in the air with your thumb sticking out while your right hand is on the mat. Once you've placed your right hand on the mat, turn your head towards your left and gaze at the tip of your left thumb as best you can.

Be careful not to strain yourself. You may not be able to turn your neck as far as needed or keep your eyes from straining to see your thumb. So, *feel your sensations* and love your body, by relaxing as much as you can while adjusting the pose to reach just 4% past your edge of discomfort.

If you *are* flexible enough to fully follow the instructions for your first exhalation without reaching the threshold of 4% beyond your edge of discomfort, spread your legs just a bit further and see if you can reach that threshold with a wider stance.

As you inhale once more, come back to the same standing posture that you began with. Then, for your second exhalation, switch directions so that you place your *left hand* in front of your right foot and turn your head to the right to gaze at the tip of your right thumb.

Up until now, the count you've been using to keep track of your breaths has been incrementing quite simply from 1 to 10. But, as you switch between the left-handed and right-handed variations of this step, begin with a count of 1 for the left side and 1 for the right side. So, instead of counting to 10 as 1, 2, 3, and so on, you'll be counting to 10 as 1, 1, 2, 2, 3, 3, and so forth.

REMEMBER, YOUR BREATHING EXERCISE IS THE MOST IMPORTANT PART OF YOUR PRACTICE!

So, be sure to maintain your breathing exercise the same way you did in Step 9.

Steps

	FOCUS	MOVEMENT	BREATH
1	Feel your sensations	Standing straight	Stage 1
2	Feel your emotions	Forward Folding	Stage 2
3	Feel your cycles	L Position	Stage 3
4	Feel your self	Arms behind & fold	Stage 4
5	Feel your relationships	Downward dog & splits	Stage 5
6	Feel your world	Head rolling	Stage 6
7	Love life	Torso extending	Loving
8	Love yourself	Hip revolving	Loving
9	Love the contrasts	Torso rotating	Loving
10	Love beauty	T twisting	Loving

Beyond

As always, be sure to do your practice *every day*, for 7 days, before starting Week 11. Outside of your practice, remember to *love beauty,* by feeling and loving the beauty of life as it is. Whether or not it's difficult for you to feel the beauty of your life, you can always love beauty by *creating* beauty. And, if you ever have any difficulty with your day, just remember to practice your breathing exercise and "Feel. Love. Now…"

QUESTIONS

Every day, after you do the practice portion of this week's lesson, ask yourself these questions and discover what answers are true for you in the moment.

- How does it feel to love beauty?

- Are you choosing to live a beautiful life?

- Did you change the pace of your breathing during your practice?

- Are you judging things as beautiful based on what others deem as beautiful?

- How easy is it for you to love beauty?

- How much do you enjoy creating beauty?

- How easy is it for you to witness the beauty of love?

- How easy is it for you to witness the beauty of life?

- How much beauty have you created today?

- Are you feeling more stable and at peace than you were before today's practice?

- Are you feeling freer than you were before today's practice and, if not, what's in the way of you feeling freer?

- Did you start to get off balance during the practice?

- Did you lose track of your breathing exercise during the practice?

- Are you scared of being beautiful?

- Are you in love with the beauty of what is?

REVIEW

After answering the list of questions on the *seventh day*, see how much you've mastered this week's lesson by observing whether you've come to realize or understand these key insights:

* Love is *beautiful*.

* Feeling love allows you to feel the beauty of what *is*.

* In the eyes of a loving parent, a child is *always* beautiful.

* Beauty is the combination of an entity's aspects that you feel as *pleasurable*.

* What pleases you is what you *allow* yourself to be pleased by.

* Pleasure results from your desires being *fulfilled*.

* Love is a *knowing and desire* to create wellness.

* Truly *understanding* love requires discipline.

* We *love* what we consider beautiful and consider beautiful what we love.

* Since you feel both beauty and love, your body knows them as *connected*.

* Artificially decreased pain and increased pleasure *tricks* your body into believing you're in love.

* Your body's confusion between love and pleasurable stimulation is a basis for *addiction*.

* *Elevate* from addiction to preference to acceptance.

* We seek less pain and more pleasure *in place of* the life we're unwilling to feel.

* The desire you feel when you're deeply in love is the *strongest* attraction possible.

* There are different *types* of desire, such as needs, wants, and love.

* There are different *degrees* of acceptance: such as hoping, believing, and knowing.

* Knowing does *not* require language.

* Knowing requires *allowing* the revealing of life.

* Being in love with your *real* life frees you from addiction.

* Expanding your capacity to love requires *discipline*.

* Opening to *real* love in place of artificial substitutes is *essential* to creating wellness and stability.

* You influence yourself and others *subconsciously*.

* By living a beautiful life of love, you *utilize* your subconscious to create wellness.

* A life filled with love is a *beautiful* life.

* A life filled with beauty is a life to be *loved*.

* People deeply enjoy creating and *sharing* in beauty.

* You are a creator, *not* just a consumer, of beauty.

FEEL. LOVE. NOW...

✳ Deep enjoyment acts as an *invitation* to love.

✳ Your femininity is *attractive*, desires to be beautiful, and desires to be loved.

✳ Your masculinity is *attracted*, desires to witness beauty, and desires to love.

✳ Your femininity feels the beauty and love of *form*.

✳ Your masculinity feels the beauty and love of *function*.

✳ To love beauty is to increase the *ability* of things to be pleasurable.

✳ Beauty is *not* linked with perfection.

✳ In love, something is beautiful *no matter* how perfect or imperfect it may be.

✳ Perfection *itself* can be imperfect – just as imperfection can be perfect as it is.

✳ To seek perfection is to seek the *solution* of all your problems.

✳ Surrender to the perfection of your *being*.

✳ To love the beauty of life is to love the beauty of *what is*.

✳ In truth, it's *all* beautiful, just as it is.

✳ Resisting the love of beauty is *futile*.

✳ Relaxation is *key*.

✳ Relax and learn while *loving* each moment.

Love
One Another

UNDERSTANDING

Who do you love? Who *don't* you love?

Since separation is an illusion of the mind, when you choose to love another what you're *actually* choosing is to love an extension of you. This is because in reality there is no "them" – only us. So, let go of any contractive-ness or hesitation you may feel in loving *anyone*, anywhere, at any time!

Of course, loving anyone, anywhere, at any time does *not* grant you the right to force yourself upon anyone – nor to force anyone to *do* anything. Since love is a knowing and desire to increase the ability to function of whatever is being loved and "to love" is to act in support of that knowing and desire, loving *anyone* requires you to honor their *freedom* by honoring their sovereignty.

This is because sovereignty is the *ultimate authority* to make choices and decisions. So, to honor a person's sovereignty is to honor the fact that each person has the ultimate authority to make choices and decisions *for themselves.*

WHENEVER YOU DENY THE SOVEREIGNTY OF ANOTHER, YOU AREN'T LOVING THEM; YOU'RE ABUSING THEM — AND ABUSE IS NEVER LOVING.

When your physical sovereignty is denied, it's physical abuse. When your mental sovereignty is denied, it's mental abuse. When your emotional sovereignty is denied, it's emotional abuse. When your sexual sovereignty is denied, it's sexual abuse.

As abuse is the *misuse* of something, it may seem as though abuse is always due to ill intent. But, that's *not* necessarily the case. In fact, it's possible to have *beautiful* intentions... all while denying the authority of others to make choices and decisions for themselves. You are even able to abuse *yourself,* with the best of intentions. Yet, in every case, to deny someone's sovereignty is to deny them love by *requiring them* to decrease their ability to function.

Of course, honoring another's sovereignty does *not* require you to dishonor your own. You can always choose differently from others. You can even go directly against another's choices with love, such as to prevent harm.

THE *KEY* TO LOVING ONE ANOTHER
ISN'T TO FACILITATE THE BEHAVIORS OF OTHERS
BUT RATHER TO NEVER STOP LOVING.

If you look at the behavior of most children (and more than a few adults) it's clear that we as human beings like to have "our way". We desire to be free, to play, learn, and explore as *we* choose. We want to receive whatever resources we believe to be lacking in our lives. And, if what we're lacking involves *someone else's* toys, it's natural for us to learn about others' sovereignty in the process of our maturing.

Learning to honor the *sovereignty* of one another is essential to learning how to *love* one another. And, honoring others requires us to be *aware* of others. In the process of maturing, we first become aware of our individual selves. Only later do we become increasingly aware of others in relationship, then in community, in society, and beyond. This is how we are able to grow from a life of selfishness to a life of love.

The level of maturity you act from in each moment shapes your ego, which serves as a mask that you wear when interacting with others. This mask is flexible and is formed, deformed, and reformed throughout your life. Self esteem is the *wellness* of your ego, meaning how well your ego is able to function in representing yourself to others.

When you are ashamed or doubting yourself, you deform your ego so that others can't see your authentic self. When you judge yourself inaccurately, you form and display an inauthentic ego to hide your strengths or weaknesses from others.

Because egos are flexible, they're inherently fragile and require both maintenance and care. Often we desire acknowledgement and validation from others to let us know what shape our masks are in, since we can't see them clearly while we're wearing them. Yet, you are always ultimately responsible for yourself, including the shape and condition of your ego. This is why self awareness is *essential* for your ego to be well enough to serve you in loving others.

The growth of your *awareness* is part of the growth of your *nervous system*, which transforms throughout your life as you continue to learn. Given that your nervous system continues to grow and adapt as you increase the embodiment of your consciousness, it's entirely natural for your body to require a good 18 *weeks* of learning to "Feel. Love. Now...". In comparison, your growth into adulthood required a good 18 *years* of learning, assuming that you received the necessary assistance and guidance from loving parents.

When learning to love one another, the importance of having received love from your parents and other caregivers can *never* be understated. This is because parental love *exists* to increase the ability of children to function. So, the less love a child receives from her or his caregivers, the less that child learns to love themselves and others – and the more that child needs to be loved in order to grow into the full physical, emotional, mental, and spiritual maturity that she or he *requires* in order to function fully and freely in life as an adult.

For those of us who received less love than we needed, in order to be able to grow to our fullest capacity, our need for love may be greater than we wish to admit. So, when loving one another, let go of judging *anyone* as needing too much to be worth loving and, instead, just *love them anyway.*

Of course, this doesn't mean that you must drop everything you're doing to give and attend to the needy. Because your attention and other resources are limited, the most loving thing you can do is to first *love yourself* so that you can love others using the *surplus* you have available to you. Only then is it loving to give your surplus resources to those who depend on you most. Indeed, this is why it's so vital that parents and other caregivers be well-resourced *in themselves.*

It's important to understand that, while *attention* is limited, love is *not.*

So, love one another by *loving them anyway.* Acknowledge them. Bless them. It doesn't take much time or effort to give love of great value. Wishing others well *shares* your love, by sharing your desire for their wellness.

The more you love *yourself* and love one another, the more you inspire others to love *themselves* and love one another as well. What one wants from others is *often* what one wants from oneself. So to love one another, *feel deeply* into what it is that you want from others and see how you can give it *to yourself.* Ask others what resources *they* desire so as to increase *their* ability to function and see what you can give them from your surplus.

As you *feel* ever more deeply and *love* ever more deeply, you will discover that you are ever more present, here and *now*. The more you *love one another*, the more you'll discover that the more you *feel into others*, the less need there is to talk. You will come to *know* how to love them in each moment, as there *is* no "them", only us.

Practice

Goal

The goal for this week is to relax, practice a vinyasa, and love one another.

Breath

For this week's portion of your breathing exercise, continue to breathe love as you did in last week's portion.

Movement

Step 11 marks a major transition from the prior steps of your movement exercise! While continuing your breathing exercise, come down onto your knees, with your feet and toes extended. Have the tips of your toes touch the *edge* of the base of your mat. Then, curl your toes and sit on your heels.

With your head and back straight and upright, extend your arms out from your sides and bend your elbows so that your hands are pointed straight up. If it helps you, you can imagine that your head is a large beachball that you're holding evenly atop your shoulders. Have your palms face each other and bring your elbows toward your back until you reach 4% past your edge of discomfort.

As sitting on your heels may create discomfort in your feet, adjust the pose as needed so that your feet are also no more than 4% past your edge of discomfort as you both inhale *and* exhale for your first count.

Then, on your next inhalation, extend your arms in front of you and uncurl your toes. Place your hands and elbows down onto your mat, so that your forehead touches the mat between your hands.

On your second exhalation, leave your hands roughly where they were on the mat and sit back on or between your heels. Relax your 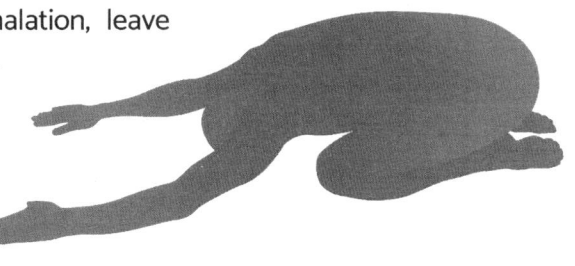 body completely and rest your forehead once more on the mat. This pose allows you to relax every part of your body. So, see if there's any place where you're still holding tension and release as much tension as you can.

On your third inhalation, use your hands to help you in extending your body face-down, with your head 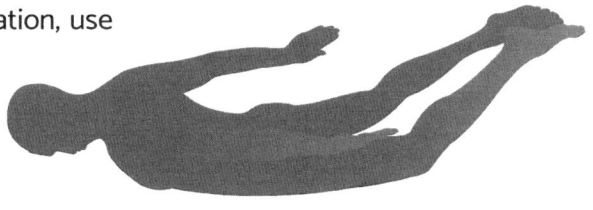 at the top and your feet near the base of your mat. With your elbows near your hips, lift your head, shoulders, arms, and legs up and away from your mat as much as you're able to, without going more than 4% past your edge of discomfort. Have your head facing straight down in order to avoid straining your neck. This position naturally results in an arching of your body, sort of like the bottom of a rocking chair.

On your third exhalation, curl your toes, place your hands on your mat near the bottom of your ribs, and push yourself back to sit on your heels once more. Then, begin a new cycle with the same instructions you followed for your first inhalation.

THIS CYCLE IS TRADITIONALLY KNOWN IN YOGIC PRACTICES AS A *VINYASA.*

Similar to how you counted 1, 1, 2, 2, and so on for Step 10, for Step 11 you'll be counting 1, 1, 1, 2, 2, 2, and so forth until you complete a count of 10.

Even though there's plenty of complexity to distract you, remember to maintain your breathing exercise as you have since Step 7. Also, be sure to do your practice *every day*, for 7 days, before starting Week 12.

Steps

	FOCUS	MOVEMENT	BREATH
1	Feel your sensations	Standing straight	Stage 1
2	Feel your emotions	Forward Folding	Stage 2
3	Feel your cycles	L Position	Stage 3
4	Feel your self	Arms behind & fold	Stage 4
5	Feel your relationships	Downward dog & splits	Stage 5
6	Feel your world	Head rolling	Stage 6
7	Love life	Torso extending	Loving
8	Love yourself	Hip revolving	Loving
9	Love the contrasts	Torso rotating	Loving
10	Love beauty	T twisting	Loving
11	Love one another	Vinyasa	Loving

Beyond

Outside of your practice, remember to *love one another*. If you ever have any difficulty in loving anyone, anywhere, at any time, simply practice your breathing exercise and "Feel. Love. Now..."

QUESTIONS

Every day, after you do the practice portion of this week's lesson, ask yourself these questions and discover what answers are true for you in the moment.

- How does it feel to love one another?

- Are you experiencing abuse in your life?

- Are you abusing either yourself or others?

- How easy is it for you to love anyone, anywhere, at any time?

- Are you well-resourced within yourself?

- Did you feel overwhelmed by the complexity of this step of your practice?

- Are you feeling more stable and at peace than you were before today's practice?

- Are you feeling freer than you were before today's practice and, if not, what's in the way of you feeling freer?

- Did you lose track of your breathing exercise during the practice?

- Did you change the pace of your breath during the practice?

- Did you start to get off balance during the practice?

- Are you afraid of loving others?

- Are you in love with *all* of us?

REVIEW

After answering the list of questions on the *seventh day*, see how much you've mastered this week's lesson by observing whether you've come to realize or understand these key insights:

* When you love another, you're actually loving an extension of *yourself.*

* You are capable of loving *anyone*, anywhere, at any time.

* Loving others does not grant you the right to *force* yourself upon them.

* Loving others does not grant you the right to force them to *do* anything.

* Truly *understanding* love requires discipline.

* Loving others requires you to honor their *sovereignty.*

* Sovereignty is the *ultimate authority* to make choices and decisions.

* To deny someone's sovereignty is to *abuse* them.

* When physical sovereignty is denied, it's *physical* abuse.

* When mental sovereignty is denied, it's *mental* abuse.

* When emotional sovereignty is denied, it's *emotional* abuse.

* When sexual sovereignty is denied, it's *sexual* abuse.

* Sexuality is not dangerous; *abuse* is dangerous.

* Abuse is *not* necessarily due to ill intent.

* You are able to abuse *yourself* while having the best of intentions.

* To deny someone's sovereignty is to deny their freedom to make *choices.*

* Denying sovereignty denies *love* by requiring a decrease in the ability to function.

* Honoring another's sovereignty *never* requires you to dishonor your own.

* The *key* to loving one another is to never stop loving.

* Loving one another is not about who but rather *how* you choose to love.

* Learning to honor one's sovereignty is *essential* to learning how to love.

* Honoring others requires you to be *aware* of others.

* Increasing *awareness* is how you grow from a life of selfishness to a life of love.

* Your process of *maturing* is the process of increasing your awareness.

* The level of maturity you act from shapes your *ego.*

* Your ego serves as a *mask* that you wear when interacting with others.

FEEL. LOVE. NOW...

✳ Your ego is *flexible* and is formed, deformed, and reformed throughout your life.

✳ Self esteem is the *wellness* of your ego.

✳ When ashamed or in doubt, you *deform* your ego so others can't see your authentic self.

✳ Egos are displayed *inauthentically* to hide strengths and weaknesses.

✳ Because egos are *flexible*, they require both maintenance and care.

✳ Often we desire *acknowledgement* in order to know what shape our masks are in.

✳ Requiring validation from others denies that we are *responsible* for our egos.

✳ Self awareness is *essential* for your ego to be well.

✳ The growth of your awareness is part of the growth of your *nervous system*.

✳ You are experiencing the *maturing* of consciousness within your body.

✳ Maturity involves *discerning* what is you and yours from what is not.

✳ Looking to see what you can get away with is a sign of *immaturity*.

✳ Immaturity limits the *extent* of your ability to love.

✳ *Trying* to speed up your maturation actually slows it down.

✳ Your *maturation* is how aware you are of what is beyond your sense of self.

✳ 18 weeks of learning to "Feel. Love. Now..." are needed to give your nervous system time to grow and *adapt.*

✳ With *loving support,* 18 years of learning are needed for children to grow their nervous systems in wellness.

✳ The importance of loving support from parents and other caregivers can *never* be understated.

✳ Parental love *exists* to increase the ability of children to function.

✳ Emotional needs for love are as important as *dietary* needs.

✳ If you received *less* love than you needed, your need for love may be greater than you wish to admit.

✳ Love itself is *without* need.

✳ Love cannot *flow* with neediness, jealousy, or expectation.

✳ Choose to be a *caregiver* rather than a caretaker.

✳ Be open to receive the gifts that you *give.*

✳ Your *responsibility* is to give the love you have to give, not to ensure that others receive it.

✳ Let go of judging *anyone* as unworthy of love and, instead, love them anyway.

FEEL. LOVE. NOW...

✳ The challenge in each moment is in loving someone who *isn't* loving you.

✳ Your attention and other resources are *limited*.

✳ Expanding your capacity to love requires *discipline*.

✳ Love yourself so that you can love others using the *surplus* you have available.

✳ It's vital for parents and other caregivers to be well-resourced *in themselves*.

✳ While attention is limited, *love* is not.

✳ It *doesn't* take much time or effort to give love of great value.

✳ Loving yourself and others inspires others to *also* love themselves and others.

✳ Feel what it is you *want* from others and see how you can give that to yourself.

✳ Give to others from your surplus based on what *they* desire.

✳ The more you *feel* into others, the less need there is to talk.

✳ By feeling into others, you come to *know* how to love them in each moment.

✳ Resisting your love for others is *futile*.

✳ Relaxation is *key*.

✳ Relax and learn while *loving* each moment.

Love
Each Moment

Understanding

It's one of love's most fascinating facts that you can only feel and love *each moment*. If you try to feel and love the past, you're trying to love a memory. If you try to feel and love the future, you're trying to love a fantasy. This is because it is *only* in each moment that you are able to experience reality. So, what *is* reality?

Reality is that which *functions*.

This means that, if something is *not* capable of functioning, it *isn't real.* Words, songs, images, thoughts, numbers, colors, and all the other ideas that you experience in your mind *aren't real.* In fact, they all qualify as unreal due to their *inability* to do anything on their own. This is true even though you *experience them* in your mind and *use them* in your life.

The reason you're able to use and experience unreal things *so vividly* is that everything that's not real is a *pattern*, which your mind uses to know *how to function*. For example, consider this sentence. At this very moment, your mind is receiving patterns in the form of words – which your mind is using to *understand* the meaning of the sentence. This sentence *itself* is also a pattern, as is this paragraph, as is this lesson, as is this program – as is your memory of the past minute, of the past year, and of your past in its *entirety*.

Even more surprisingly, the way that unreal things are used to direct *real things* to function isn't limited to your mind. In fact, it's the basis of *everything* you experience. It's the basis of every art, every science, and every technology. It's how you are able to feel, how life is able to live, and how *you* are able to love!

TO *TRULY* LOVE,
IT'S NECESSARY TO UNDERSTAND
WHAT IS REAL AND WHAT IS NOT.

Because love is a knowing and desire to increase the *ability to function* of whatever is being loved and "to love" is to *act* in support of that knowing and desire, you can *only* love things that function. In other words, you can only love *what's real*. If you instead try to love something that is *unreal*, you are experiencing attachment to your *imagination* rather than real love.

Thankfully, *you* function. So, you can be loved. Other people function. So, they can be loved. Families, communities, and societies function. Businesses, machines, and infrastructure function. Animals, plants, and even rocks function. They may not be doing much but rocks *are* able to do something, even if only to function as paperweights. Indeed, *all of reality* functions. And so, all of reality is available to be loved *by you* in each moment.

Since the past is an idea in the form of memory and the future is an idea in the form of fantasy, reality *only* exists in the present moment because it is *only* in the present moment that *anything* functions. This means that to love each moment is to *love your reality.*

Of course, since what you experience as love provides you with a knowing and a desire, love is something you can only *feel* in the present moment. And, since neither a knowing nor a desire can do anything on its own, knowledge and desires *aren't real.* However, because they aren't real, knowledge and desires qualify as *patterns* that you can use to direct yourself in *how* you function.

INDEED, LOVE PROVIDES YOU WITH THE *PATTERNS* YOU NEED TO FOLLOW *IN EACH MOMENT* IN ORDER TO CREATE *WELLNESS.*

This is how love functions – and how you know that love is real. You see, love is infinite. So, loving is never over and done with. Instead, loving is something you do in *each moment*; it's something to do right *now.* That's why this program is titled "Feel. Love. Now..." instead of "Now... Feel. Love."

When you love each moment, what you're doing is increasing the ability of reality to function. You are loving the present – which is quite a gift! It is a gift to be *alive.* It is a gift to be *loved.* It is a gift to love and be *able* to love.

You are only given the gift of reality in each moment – but what a generous gift it is! After all, how amazing is it that love *gives you* the patterns you need to follow in order to create wellness in each moment?

The gift of each moment, the gift of the *now,* is so tremendous that it will take a full 6 weeks to unwrap it! But, for the rest of *this* week, let each moment be your time to love. Use your time to love life, to love yourself, to love the contrasts, to love beauty, to love one another and, indeed, to love each moment.

PRACTICE

Goal

The goal for this week is to relax, do some push-ups, and love each moment.

Breath

For this week's portion of your breathing exercise, continue to breathe love as you did in last week's portion.

Movement

Step 12 continues where you left off with Step 11, face down on your yoga mat. As you continue your breathing exercise, place your hands on your mat with your palms underneath your shoulders. Lying there on your belly, curl your toes and breathe in for your first inhalation.

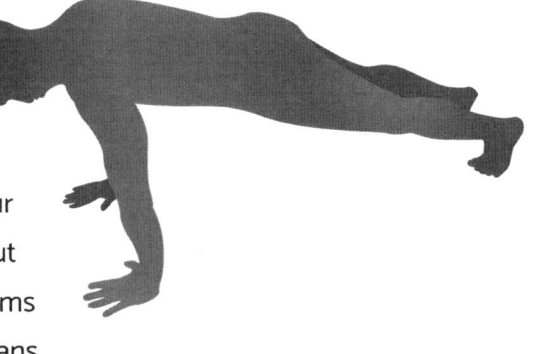

Then as you exhale, push yourself up with your body extended like a plank, so that you complete your exhalation just as you max out your ability to extend your arms *and* your shoulders. This means that you will likely be extending your shoulders *past* where you might normally end a push-up.

If you aren't strong enough yet in your upper body to push yourself up like this, place your knees down on your mat and see if you're able to push yourself up with your knees bearing some of your weight. Lifting your feet high up off your mat may help with this.

If you aren't strong enough to push yourself up from the floor while on your knees, remain in a plank position instead with your legs extended, if you can.

BE SURE TO CONTINUE YOUR BREATHING EXERCISE
EVENLY THROUGHOUT THE ENTIRE STEP
AND MAINTAIN THE SAME PACE OF BREATH
THAT YOU'VE BEEN USING
FOR THE PRIOR STEPS OF YOUR PRACTICE.

As soon as you finish your exhalation, begin your inhalation and lower yourself back down at the same pace you pushed yourself up. If you can lower yourself to *just above* your mat, please do. Otherwise, you can lower yourself all the way down, if needed.

Continue this cycle of pushing yourself up and lowering yourself down for a count of 20 breaths. Whether on the way up or the way down, *lead* your movement with your breath. Rather than distracting yourself with thoughts about the exercise, relax as much as you can, focus on your feelings, and see how it feels to love *each moment*.

Of course, it's natural for your breathing to become heavier during this exercise. However, if you aren't able to maintain the same pace and depth of breath for all 20 breaths, stop as soon as you have *difficulty* breathing. Then, remember which count you stopped at. As you continue to practice daily, you'll find that your strength and the count you stop at will naturally increase.

Steps

	FOCUS	MOVEMENT	BREATH
1	Feel your sensations	Standing straight	Stage 1
2	Feel your emotions	Forward Folding	Stage 2
3	Feel your cycles	L Position	Stage 3
4	Feel your self	Arms behind & fold	Stage 4
5	Feel your relationships	Downward dog & splits	Stage 5
6	Feel your world	Head rolling	Stage 6
7	Love life	Torso extending	Loving
8	Love yourself	Hip revolving	Loving
9	Love the contrasts	Torso rotating	Loving
10	Love beauty	T twisting	Loving
11	Love one another	Vinyasa	Loving
12	Love each moment	Push-ups	Loving

Beyond

Both inside and outside of your practice, choose to *love each moment,* by observing the things in your life that are able to function and then *supporting* their ability to do so. If you ever have any difficulty, simply practice your breathing exercise and "Feel. Love. Now…" Like always, be sure to do your practice *every day*, for 7 days, before reading the Section II Review. Also, take a moment now to notice just how far you've come!

QUESTIONS

Every day, after you do the practice portion of this week's lesson, ask yourself these questions and discover what answers are true for you in the moment.

- How does it feel to love each moment?

- Are you able to discern what's real and what's not?

- Did you feel overcome by the implications of understanding?

- How easy is it for you to love each moment?

- Are you resisting doing your daily practice?

- Did you judge yourself for having difficulty with your practice?

- Are you feeling more stable and at peace than you were before today's practice?

- Are you feeling freer than you were before today's practice and, if not, what's in the way of you feeling freer?

- Did you change the pace of your breath during your practice?

- Are you afraid of loving what's real?

- Are you in love with *each moment*?

Review

After answering the list of questions on the *seventh day*, see how much you've mastered this week's lesson by observing whether you've come to realize or understand these key insights:

✳ You can only feel and love *each moment*.

✳ If you try to love the past, you're trying to love a *memory*.

✳ If you try to love the future, you're trying to love a *fantasy*.

✳ Yesterday and tomorrow are *ideas*.

✳ Focusing on creating success in the *future* prevents success in the present.

✳ Only in each *present* moment can you experience reality.

✳ Reality is that which *functions*.

✳ If something is *not* capable of functioning, it isn't real.

✳ The things you experience in your mind *aren't real*, even though you use them.

✳ Things that aren't real are *patterns* that your mind uses to know how to function.

✳ Your external reality *reflects* your internal reality.

✳ The *interrelating* of patterns reveals the underlying functioning of reality.

* The way *unreal* things direct real things to function is the basis of life, love, and feeling.

* To *truly* love, it's necessary to understand what is real and what is not.

* Since you can only love things that function, you can only love what is *real.*

* Since reality functions, reality is able to be loved *by you* in each moment.

* As things only function in the present moment, reality only *exists* in the present.

* To *love each moment* is to love your reality.

* Reality is your *ally,* whenever you allow it to be.

* By focusing entirely on what you *like,* you ignore reality whenever you don't like it.

* In reality, love provides *patterns* for you to follow so as to create wellness in each moment.

* Loving is *never* over and done with.

* Expanding your capacity to love requires *discipline.*

* Truly *understanding* love requires discipline.

* As loving is something you do in each moment, it's something to do *right now.*

FEEL. LOVE. NOW...

✳ When you love each moment, you increase the ability of reality to *function*.

✳ Love *knows* the patterns you need to follow to create wellness in each moment.

✳ Love is more *intelligent* than your ability to think.

✳ The present moment is a gift worth *loving*.

✳ Resisting your love for each moment is *futile*.

✳ Relaxation is *key*.

✳ Relax and learn while *loving* each moment.

Love
It All

Congratulations on completing Section II!

IF YOU'VE FINISHED ALL OF THE WEEKLY LESSONS SO FAR, YOU'VE DEFINITELY LEARNED TO LOVE IN A BIG WAY!

To see just how much progress you've made, please use this opportunity to re-read the review sections for Week 7 through Week 12. As with Section I, reviewing your progress is *definitely* a worthwhile use of your time! Once you've done so, see whether you've mastered these key points and discover how much you've learned:

* All you need is *love*.

* You are *free* to love.

* You are free to *be* loved.

FEEL. LOVE. NOW...

✳ You are *blessed* to love.

✳ You are blessed to be *loved*.

✳ Life *exists* because of love.

✳ Life is the *expression* of love.

✳ Loving life requires *accepting* life.

✳ Life is *delightful* when we choose to love it.

✳ Loving life *requires you* to love yourself.

✳ Self love is *both* self actualization *and* self realization.

✳ Self love gives you *permission* to be you.

✳ Self love nurtures your body *here* in the present moment.

✳ How you love yourself *shows* others how to love you.

✳ The only obstacle to your love is your *self*.

✳ Be the greatest expression of love you can *be*.

✳ The more *mature* you are, the more *loving* you can be.

✳ The more you allow yourself to *feel* love, the more you know you *are* loved.

✳ The key to living in wellness is *acting on* love rather than fear.

✳ We are misled in *believing* that love is insufficient.

✳ Love underlies *all* of reality.

* True love is *not* something you can earn.

* The truth of love is the most *valuable* thing you can learn.

* Love people where they *are* in their development.

* No one can be *forced* to love.

* No one can be forced to *feel* loved.

* Be in service to love through the peacefulness of your *being*.

* Be in service to love through the assistance, support, and nurturing of your *doing*.

* Be in service to love through the sweetness of your *having*.

* Love is neither *thought* nor *bought*.

* You *feel* love; you cannot *think* love.

* Love reveals the intelligence of *reality*.

* Love is *beautiful*.

* Love *isn't* always pretty.

* Love is the *basis* of salvation.

* Love is *wise*.

* Love is *respectful*.

* Love is *wonderful!*

* Love is *real!*

FEEL. LOVE. NOW...

✳ Love is *not* quantifiable.

✳ Love is *infinite*.

✳ Love *gives you* the patterns to follow to create wellness in each moment.

✳ Yes, *you* are loved.

So, are you ready to love what's here and...?

Section III
NOW...

Now is Influenced by the Past

UNDERSTANDING

Because the past isn't real and you can only love reality in each moment, it may surprise you to know that being *aware* of the past can help you to create stability and wellness in your life. But to understand how, it's first necessary to understand *consciousness*. So, let's start off by defining it:

CONSCIOUSNESS IS THE ABILITY TO WITNESS AND MAKE CHOICES.

Of course, you're only able to witness and make choices in the *present* moment. So, consciousness exists in the *now*. Yet, somehow you are able to remember patterns from the *past* – even though you're *not* able to remember the future. Remembering that *reality* only exists in the present moment, *now* you can understand the relationship between consciousness and reality:

CONSCIOUSNESS IS WHAT *ENABLES* THINGS TO FUNCTION.

Consciousness is what enables you to love, by enabling reality to exist. Essentially, reality is the *expression* of consciousness. In other words, reality is consciousness *creating*. This is why consciousness is *not* in any way limited to human beings. Rather, *all* living beings are able to witness and make choices to some extent. In fact, consciousness *permeates* our Universe – and it functions by *vibrating*.

To more easily understand this, it may help you to think of consciousness as an infinite ocean of potential in the form of information. Whenever a choice is made, a *wave* is created in this ocean. These waves then infinitely interact with each other, causing incredibly detailed patterns of information to emerge in ways we recognize as things like energy, matter, space, and time. This then allows conscious beings, such as yourself, to witness those patterns and make choices that result in *more* patterns.

AS AN ASPECT OF CONSCIOUSNESS,
YOUR FREEDOM TO CHOOSE IS YOUR *FREE WILL*.

Since waves spread throughout consciousness, the effects of *past* choices can be witnessed as patterns in the *present*. Since the ocean of consciousness is infinite, there is nothing to stop the effects of past choices. It's only by there being *additional* waves that the effects of past choices can be modified or nullified to the point that their patterns become unrecognizable.

In more human terms, each present moment is always influenced by past choices. This is how you are able to remember things and how you can *learn* from past choices. Yet, the most important thing to learn from the past is to be *present*. This is because the past has passed and is not something that can be repaired or repeated. Instead, the past is something to be learned from, and sometimes healed from, with care and compassion.

By learning from the past, you are able to account for the effects of your choices. By being more responsible for the *effects* of your choices in each present moment, you are then able to *love* more effectively. Plus, by learning from the effects of past choices, you are better able to *assist* living beings as they heal from illness and injury in each moment.

As each now is *influenced* by the past, waves of consciousness allow life to flow while also allowing love to flow. So, love life through your choices in each moment, as you continually learn from the effects of choices made in the past.

PRACTICE

Goal

The goal for this week is to relax, do some cat-cow stretches, lean back, and be present with the past.

Breath

For this week's portion of your breathing exercise, continue to breathe love as you did in last week's portion.

Movement

Step 13 continues where you left off with Step 12, at the end of a push-up. As you continue your breathing exercise, get onto your knees while keeping your hands where they were. Then, rotate your palms *inward* until you begin to feel some tension in your forearms. Have your wrists be directly below your shoulders and your knees directly below your hips so that you are in a stable stance requiring minimal effort to maintain.

On your inhalation, tilt your pelvic bowl *forward* to 4% past your edge of discomfort, such that your belly dips down. This will likely cause your spine to form a U shape, possibly even bringing your head up as well.

On your exhalation, tilt your pelvic bowl *backward* to 4% past your edge of discomfort, such that your back arches up. This will cause your spine to look more like an upside-down U shape, likely bringing your head down as well.

Let your breath lead the movement of your body for a count of 10 breaths, while feeling the wave-like motion of your spine. Be sure to begin every movement from your pelvis, as it will help you to release any tension stored in your spine. Commonly, variations of this movement are called "cat-cow stretches" as they can be used to gently stretch your spine similar to how cats and cows do.

Once you've completed 10 cat-cow stretches while practicing your breathing exercise, rotate your palms *outward* until you begin to feel some tension in your forearms. Keep your wrists directly below your shoulders, with your knees directly below your hips. Then, do 10 more cat-cow stretches while practicing your breathing exercise.

Since this step of your daily practice puts some tension into your wrists and forearms, it's important for you to also *release* that tension. So, once you've completed the second set of 10 breaths, extend your toes and lean back on your ankles and lower legs, preferably with your butt between your legs on your mat. To prop yourself up, put your arms and shoulders back behind you with your arms straight and the tops of your wrists touching your mat.

Keep your back straight and adjust your position so that you're only 4% past your edge of discomfort. Then, maintain your position for 10 full breaths, as you continue your breathing exercise, and release any remaining tension you've built up in your ankles, wrists, and forearms.

Steps

	FOCUS	MOVEMENT	BREATH
1	Feel your sensations	Standing straight	Stage 1
2	Feel your emotions	Forward Folding	Stage 2
3	Feel your cycles	L Position	Stage 3
4	Feel your self	Arms behind & fold	Stage 4
5	Feel your relationships	Downward dog & splits	Stage 5
6	Feel your world	Head rolling	Stage 6
7	Love life	Torso extending	Loving
8	Love yourself	Hip revolving	Loving
9	Love the contrasts	Torso rotating	Loving
10	Love beauty	T twisting	Loving
11	Love one another	Vinyasa	Loving
12	Love each moment	Push-ups	Loving
13	Be present with the past	Cat-cow & lean back	Loving

Beyond

Outside of your practice, *be present with the past* by observing the effects of past choices. As this may be uncomfortable for you, remember to relax and *open* into the discomfort.

As always, be sure to do your practice *every day*, for 7 days, before starting Week 14. Also, if you ever experience any difficulty, simply practice your breathing exercise and "Feel. Love. Now..."

QUESTIONS

Every day, after you do the practice portion of this week's lesson, ask yourself these questions and discover what answers are true for you in the moment.

- What have you learned today from your past?

- What effects are you observing from choices you made in childhood?

- How aware are you of your own consciousness?

- Do you recognize any waves in the effects of your past choices?

- How easy is it for you to learn from the past?

- How different are your past choices from your current choices?

- How fluid is the movement of your spine?

- Are you resisting doing your practice?

- Are you relaxing into any discomfort?

- Are you feeling more stable and at peace than you were before today's practice?

- Are you feeling freer than you were before today's practice and, if not, what's in the way of you feeling freer?

- Did you change the pace of your breath during the practice?

- How does it feel to face your past?

- Are you present with your past?

REVIEW

After answering the list of questions on the *seventh day*, see how much you've mastered this week's lesson by observing whether you've come to realize or understand these key insights:

* Consciousness is the ability to *witness* and make *choices.*

* Consciousness exists in the *now.*

* You are able to witness *patterns* caused by past choices.

* Consciousness is what *enables* things to function.

* Consciousness enables you to love by enabling *reality* to exist.

* Reality is the *expression* of consciousness.

* Consciousness is *not* limited to human beings.

* *All* living beings are able to witness and make choices to some extent.

* Consciousness *permeates* our Universe.

* Our Universe is *alive.*

* Consciousness functions by *vibrating.*

* Consciousness is like an infinite ocean of *potential* in the form of information.

* Fantasy explores *ideas* in the ocean of potential.

* To be *awake* is to be aware of your experience of reality in place of fantasy.

* Being is not temporary; only your *awareness* of it is.

* Whenever a choice is made, a *wave* is created in the ocean of consciousness.

* Waves of consciousness *infinitely* interact with each other, causing patterns to emerge.

* Conscious beings witness patterns and make choices that result in *more* patterns.

* As individuals, we are only conscious of *portions* of the ocean of consciousness.

* The effects of past choices can be witnessed in the present because waves *spread* throughout consciousness.

* As an aspect of consciousness, your freedom to *choose* is your free will.

* Free will is the *reason* that you can remember the past but not the future.

* There is no end to the *effects* of past choices.

* The effects of past choices can only be altered by *additional* choices.

* Each present moment is *influenced* by past choices.

* The influence of past choices is how you are able to remember and *learn*.

* You learn by discovering "what" instead of explaining "*why*".

* ✳ "Should" is a claim of *history*.

* ✳ The past has *passed*.

* ✳ The most important thing to learn from the past is to be *present*.

* ✳ Expanding your capacity to be present requires *discipline*.

* ✳ Truly *understanding* the present requires discipline.

* ✳ The past is *not* something that can be repaired or repeated.

* ✳ The past is something to be learned from with *care* and *compassion*.

* ✳ By learning from the past, you are able to account for the *effects* of your choices.

* ✳ Being more responsible in your choices allows you to love more *effectively*.

* ✳ By learning, you are better able to assist yourself and others in *healing*.

* ✳ Waves of consciousness allow *life* to flow while also allowing love to flow.

* ✳ Love life through your choices, as you learn from the *effects* of past choices.

* ✳ Resisting the past is *futile*.

* ✳ Relaxation is *key*.

* ✳ Relax and learn while loving *each moment*.

Now is the Essence of Creation

UNDERSTANDING

Your ability to choose is your ability to create. By choosing what to do – or not to do, you influence what is created and what is destroyed in our Universe. This means that consciousness, as the ability to witness and make choices, not only enables reality to exist; consciousness is also the basis of *both* each present moment *and* creation itself.

Together with the rest of our Universe, we *create* reality through the choices we make. As each choice creates a new wave in the ocean of consciousness, choosing *is* the act and action of creation.

The waves of creation that result from the making of choices cause consciousness *itself* to vibrate. This vibration is the basis of all sound.

ESSENTIALLY, REALITY IS THE *SONG* OF CONSCIOUSNESS.

Whenever you choose to create wellness instead of illness, what you are choosing is to create harmony instead of discord. The more loving you are, the more *harmoniously* you add to life's chorus. The more conscious you are of your own consciousness, the more loving you are able to *be*.

The vibration of consciousness creates patterns through the interference of waves connecting with each other. These connections are what we experience as *meaning*.

When we choose to create patterns of meaning, we are creating *stories*. These stories are ways of witnessing our shared existence, sort of like the melody of a single instrument being played as part of an orchestra.

The vibration of consciousness is commonly referred to as "spiritual vibration". And, like all vibrations, you can distinguish spiritual vibrations by their *frequency* and their *intensity*. The frequency of a spiritual vibration is its approximation to and alignment with reality. So, the higher the spiritual frequency – the closer to reality it is, while the lower the spiritual frequency – the further from reality it is.

TRUTH IS THE *STATE* OF REALITY.

You can think of spiritual vibrations as being the oscillation of information *relative* to truth. Fortunately, truth does not require any effort on your part in order to be true! Instead, truth is something you can trust in and rest in because truth is *always* true. Truth does not exist to criticize you but rather to *direct* you to vibrate in *harmony* with reality.

IN REALITY,
WELLNESS IS ALIGNMENT WITH THE *TRUTH* OF LOVE.

Since truth is the state of reality, alignment with reality results in alignment with truth. This is why the *intensity* of a spiritual vibration is its power to influence reality. This means that, like other sounds, the stories in spiritual vibrations can vary by being either louder or quieter and having a higher or lower pitch. They can also be shortened, lengthened, and repeated. In this way, living beings are able to seek your attention by expressing themselves frequently, loudly, and/or repetitively.

By understanding that consciousness is the basis of creation in each moment, you are *now* able to understand stability. This is because stability is what you create by lengthening and repeating notes while singing the song of life. As for how to create *wellness*, that is something you do by loving life in each moment. Essentially, love *guides* your choices to create wellness universally.

FUNDAMENTALLY,
LIFE'S ORCHESTRA IS *CONDUCTED* BY LOVE.

As for how, we'll address that in the coming weeks. In the meantime, though, know that *you* are a creator. Through your choices, both past and present, you are a powerful originator of your experiences. So, marvel at your creations! And, if you'd like to create something new, do that as well. Simply create from love in each moment – and enjoy the harmony of life in wellness.

PRACTICE

Goal

The goal for this week is to relax, squat, and be present with creation.

Breath

For this week's portion of your breathing exercise, continue to breathe love as you did in last week's portion.

Movement

For Step 14 of your daily practice, come into a squatting position. Place your heels directly below your shoulders with your feet facing forward. Keep your head and back straight, place your palms together, and have the outer part of your arms touch the inner part of your knees or thighs. You can have your knees spread as wide as you like. If it increases your stability to create pressure between your elbows and inner knees, you're welcome to do so.

Balance on the *arches* of your feet, between the heel and ball of each foot. Then, adjust your position so that you're only 4% past your edge of discomfort. If possible, have your heels placed firmly on your mat.

If you discover that you're so flexible that you're not *able* to be 4% past your edge of discomfort then you can flip your squat upside down, in what is commonly known as "Happy Baby" pose. In this pose, you lie on your back while raising your knees to the outer sides of your chest. With your legs forming roughly an L shape as seen from your right side, place your hands on or near your heels and pull your heels towards your mat and towards your head. Make sure that the back of your pelvis is touching the mat and your knees are not strained as you adjust your position so that you're 4% past your edge of discomfort.

Whether you're squatting down or squatting up, in "Happy Baby" pose, be sure to relax every part of your body that isn't required to hold the pose, especially your anus and pelvic muscles. Then, do your breathing exercise for a count of 20 breaths, choosing to create relaxation in place of any unnecessary tension.

Steps

	FOCUS	MOVEMENT	BREATH
1	Feel your sensations	Standing straight	Stage 1
2	Feel your emotions	Forward Folding	Stage 2
3	Feel your cycles	L Position	Stage 3
4	Feel your self	Arms behind & fold	Stage 4
5	Feel your relationships	Downward dog & splits	Stage 5
6	Feel your world	Head rolling	Stage 6
7	Love life	Torso extending	Loving
8	Love yourself	Hip revolving	Loving
9	Love the contrasts	Torso rotating	Loving
10	Love beauty	T twisting	Loving
11	Love one another	Vinyasa	Loving
12	Love each moment	Push-ups	Loving
13	Be present with the past	Cat-cow & lean back	Loving
14	Be present with creation	Squatting	Loving

Beyond

Outside of your practice, *be present with creation* by observing what it is that you and the rest of our Universe are creating. As this may bring up some discomfort for you, remember to relax and *open* into the discomfort. If you ever have any difficulty, simply practice your breathing exercise and "Feel. Love. Now..." As always, be sure to do your practice *every day*, for 7 days, before starting Week 15.

QUESTIONS

Every day, after you do the practice portion of this week's lesson, ask yourself these questions and discover what answers are true for you in the moment.

- What have you created today?

- How easy is it for you to be responsible for your creations?

- Have your choices been in harmony with life today?

- Are your spiritual vibrations having a high frequency?

- Are your spiritual vibrations having a high intensity?

- Do you like what it is that you're creating?

- Are you resisting doing your daily practice?

- Are you relaxing into any discomfort?

- Are you feeling more stable and at peace than you were before today's practice?

- Are you feeling freer than you were before today's practice and, if not, what's in the way of you feeling freer?

- Are you waking up to truth?

- How does it feel to create your life?

- Are you present with creation?

REVIEW

After answering the list of questions on the *seventh day*, see how much you've mastered this week's lesson by observing whether you've come to realize or understand these key insights:

* ✳ The ability to choose *is* the ability to create.

* ✳ Your choices *influence* what is created and destroyed in our Universe.

* ✳ Consciousness is the basis of *both* each present moment and creation itself.

* ✳ You *create* much of your reality through the choices you make.

* ✳ Choosing is the act and *action* of creation.

* ✳ Waves of creation cause consciousness *itself* to vibrate.

* ✳ The vibration of consciousness is the basis of all *sound*.

* ✳ Reality is the *song* of consciousness.

* ✳ To create wellness in place of illness is to create *harmony* in place of *discord*.

* ✳ The more loving you are, the more *harmoniously* you add to life's chorus.

* ✳ The more conscious you are, the more loving you are able to *be*.

* ✳ The vibration of consciousness creates *patterns* of connections between waves.

✳ Patterns of connections in consciousness are what you experience as *meaning.*

✳ Patterns of meaning are what you experience as *stories.*

✳ Stories are ways of *witnessing* our shared existence.

✳ Stories are like the melody of an instrument being *played* as part of an orchestra.

✳ *Spiritual* vibration is the vibration of consciousness.

✳ You can distinguish *all* vibrations by their frequency and their intensity.

✳ The *frequency* of a spiritual vibration is its approximation to and alignment with reality.

✳ The *intensity* of a spiritual vibration is its *power* to influence reality.

✳ We resonate unconsciously at the spiritual frequency of the *collective.*

✳ Conscious choice is required to vibrate at a *higher* frequency than the collective.

✳ Alignment with reality results in alignment with *truth.*

✳ Truth is the *state* of reality.

✳ Truth does not need to be *proved.*

✳ Truth is something you can *trust* in and *rest* in, because truth is always true.

* Acceptance of truth requires *relaxing*.

* Truth is *not* punishment.

* Truth is the antidote for *illness*.

* Wellness is alignment with the truth of *love*.

* Stability is what you create by *extending* and *repeating* notes while singing the song of life.

* The orchestra of life is conducted by *love*.

* You are a *creator*.

* Through your choices, you are a powerful *originator* of your experiences.

* You are responsible for your choices, *not* your circumstances.

* Create wellness by creating with love in *each* present moment.

* Expanding your capacity to be present requires *discipline*.

* Truly *understanding* the present requires discipline.

* Resisting creation is *futile*.

* Relaxation is *key*.

* Relax and learn while loving *each moment*.

Now is the Flow of Life

UNDERSTANDING

Have you ever noticed how richly detailed and complex life is? From the largest scales to the smallest, the vibration of consciousness powers the *intricacies* of the cycles of life. As life *itself* is constantly vibrating, the cycles of life are the waves within waves within waves... that bring about the elegant complexity of life's flow.

The rich elegance of life is a result of the *fractal* nature of reality. You may remember having seen images of fractal *geometry* in the form of richly detailed outputs of mathematical formulae. But in fact, fractals are *everywhere.*

THIS IS BECAUSE FRACTALS ARE PATTERNS
THAT EXHIBIT *SIMILARITY*
BETWEEN A WHOLE AND ITS PARTS.

Inherently, fractals result from the infinite vibrations of vibrations of vibrations... of consciousness. You can see fractals with your own eyes by looking at the branches of a tree or in the way that rivers form. You might notice fractals in the shapes of mountains, clouds, and sand dunes. Essentially, every pattern that results from the growth and diminishment of life's flow is a fractal.

Because fractals are a result of the vibration of consciousness, they're not limited to just shapes. In fact, they exist throughout *every* aspect of reality, including what we perceive as time. This means that *each moment* is far richer in complexity than anyone will *ever* be able to understand. This fact is why the present is such a precious gift!

The fractal flowering and flowing of life is a result of the cyclical unfolding of nature. As a mother gives birth to a child who gives birth to a child who gives birth to a child for as long as there are children, you are part of the unfolding of humanity. And, humanity is merely a *child* of our Mother Earth.

YOU ARE AN ASPECT OF LIFE *ITSELF*,
WHICH IS INTELLIGENT AND SELF-AWARE.

As *human* beings, we are *living* beings, collectively forming a *species* that we call "humanity". And, because species are made up of living beings, they are *themselves* alive.

As individuals, we are *multicellular* organisms, meaning that each of us is composed of many cells. Each of us is a living being because each of our *cells* is a living being.

There are many species of living beings that live *with us* in our world. There are also many living beings that live *in and on* us, such as bacteria, archaea, fungi, and other living beings. Just like the living beings in and on *your body*, the beings that live with us in and on *our world* must cooperate in order for our world to be well.

Because of the fractal nature of reality, we are like cells of the bodies of larger living beings, which are themselves like cells of *even larger* living beings, which are like cells of even larger living beings, and so on. Indeed, you and I are very much like bacteria on the skin of our Mother Earth, which is like a cell in the body of our galaxy, which is like a cell in the body of our Universe. Yet, each of us is a unique individual.

YOUR UNIQUE AND INDIVIDUAL PORTION OF CONSCIOUSNESS IS YOUR *SOUL*.

Because of the fractal nature of reality, your soul is part of a collective called an *oversoul*. Your oversoul is then part of even *larger* soul collective, which is part of an even larger soul collective and so on. The fractal totality of soul collectives is the totality of consciousness *itself* – and that totality is the entirety of our Universe of multiverses, otherwise known by a multitude of names such as Source, Great Spirit, and God.

ALONG WITH THE REST OF SOURCE,
WE FORM A SINGLE LIVING ORGANISM
THAT IS OUR UNIVERSE IN ITS *ENTIRETY*.

So, now you know; reality is God expressing *ourself* in each moment. As expressions of life itself, we are infinitely flowing and flowering in form. And yet, we are also each a witness and creator of our own choices. In each moment, we flow together as a single living being, a *Universe*. That is why *now* is the flow of life.

PRACTICE

Goal

The goal for this week is to relax, do some sit-ups, and be present with life's flow.

Breath

For this week's portion of your breathing exercise, continue to breathe love as you did in last week's portion.

Movement

For Step 15 of your daily practice, come onto your back if you aren't already and bend your legs. With your knees pointed towards the ceiling, place the soles of your feet on your mat. Extend your arms towards your feet and then bend your *elbows* so that your elbows are positioned near your waist with your hands pointing upwards.

Remain on your back for your first inhalation and then start to sit up with a straight back on your first *exhalation*, leading with your chest. As you sit up, adjust the angle of your knees and both the angle and elevation of your elbows so that your sit-up is only 4% past your edge of discomfort. Keeping your heels on your mat, be sure to finish sitting up at the same time that you complete your exhalation.

On your second inhalation, gently lower yourself back down so that the backs of your *shoulders* reach your mat at the end of your inhalation. Then, begin another sit-up on your next exhalation for a count of 20 breaths. If you find that you're not able to adjust yourself to complete 20 sit-ups at 4% past your edge of discomfort, simply do as many as you can.

BE SURE TO RELAX ANY PART OF YOUR BODY WHERE TENSION ISN'T REQUIRED TO COMPLETE EACH SIT-UP.

Like always, your breathing exercise is the most important part of your practice. So, focus on keeping your breathing slow, deep, and even as you remain present with the flow of life.

Steps

	FOCUS	MOVEMENT	BREATH
1	Feel your sensations	Standing straight	Stage 1
2	Feel your emotions	Forward Folding	Stage 2
3	Feel your cycles	L Position	Stage 3
4	Feel your self	Arms behind & fold	Stage 4
5	Feel your relationships	Downward dog & splits	Stage 5
6	Feel your world	Head rolling	Stage 6
7	Love life	Torso extending	Loving
8	Love yourself	Hip revolving	Loving
9	Love the contrasts	Torso rotating	Loving
10	Love beauty	T twisting	Loving
11	Love one another	Vinyasa	Loving
12	Love each moment	Push-ups	Loving
13	Be present with the past	Cat-cow & lean back	Loving
14	Be present with creation	Squatting	Loving
15	Be present with life's flow	Sit-ups	Loving

Beyond

Outside of your practice, *be present with life's flow* by observing similarities in your everyday life between a whole and its parts. In the process, you'll discover that the fractal flow of life is noticeable in each moment, everywhere you look.

If you ever have any difficulty, simply practice your breathing exercise and "Feel. Love. Now…" Also, be sure to do your practice *every day*, for 7 days, before starting Week 16.

QUESTIONS

Every day, after you do the practice portion of this week's lesson, ask yourself these questions and discover what answers are true for you in the moment.

- How is life's flow flowering in this moment?

- Are you witnessing the fractal nature of your existence?

- Are you grateful for the unfolding of your life?

- Are you accepting yourself for who and what you are?

- Are you loving the flow of life?

- Are you resisting doing your daily practice?

- Are you relaxing into any discomfort?

- Are you feeling more stable and at peace than you were before today's practice?

- Are you feeling freer than you were before today's practice and, if not, what's in the way of you feeling freer?

- Are you waking up to the truth of each moment?

- How does the flowering of life feel to you?

- Are you present with life's flow?

REVIEW

After answering the list of questions on the *seventh day*, see how much you've mastered this week's lesson by observing whether you've come to realize or understand these key insights:

* ✳ The vibration of consciousness *powers* the cycles of life.

* ✳ The cycles of life are the waves within waves of life's *flow*.

* ✳ The flow of life is the flow of *information*.

* ✳ Love is a flow of information directing life towards *wellness*.

* ✳ The elegance of life is a result of the *fractal* nature of reality.

* ✳ Fractals are *everywhere*.

* ✳ Fractals are patterns that exhibit *similarity* between a whole and its parts.

* ✳ Fractals result from the infinite vibrations of *vibrations* of consciousness.

* ✳ Every *pattern* resulting from the growth or diminishment of life's flow is a fractal.

* ✳ Fractals exist throughout *every* aspect of reality, including time.

* ✳ Each moment is far more *complex* than anyone will ever be able to understand.

* ✳ The fractal flowing of *life* is a result of the cyclical unfolding of our Universe.

✳ Our Universe shows you *reflections* of yourself in the situations of others.

✳ You are part of the *unfolding* of humanity.

✳ You are an aspect of life *itself*, which is intelligent and self-aware.

✳ Expanding your capacity to be present and self-aware requires *discipline*.

✳ Truly *understanding* the present requires discipline.

✳ As human beings, we are living beings that form a *species* called "humanity".

✳ Because species are made up of living beings, they are *themselves* alive.

✳ We are *multicellular* organisms, meaning each of us is composed of many cells.

✳ Each of your cells is a living being, which is why *you* are a living being.

✳ There are many species of living beings that live *with us* in our world.

✳ There are many living beings that live *in and on* us.

✳ The beings that live in and on *our world* must cooperate for our world to be well.

✳ We are like the *cells* of larger living beings, which are like the cells of *even larger* living beings.

✳ We are like bacteria on the *skin* of our Mother Earth, which is like a cell of our galaxy, which is like a cell of our Universe.

✳ We are all *aspects* of the same organism.

✳ Each of us is a *unique* individual.

✳ Your unique and individual expression of consciousness is your *soul*.

✳ Because reality is fractal, your soul is part of a *collective* of collectives.

✳ The fractal *totality* of soul collectives is the totality of consciousness itself.

✳ The totality of consciousness is our *Universe*, also known as God.

✳ Along with the rest of God, we form a single living organism that *is* our Universe.

✳ Reality is God expressing *ourself* in each moment.

✳ As expressions of life itself, we are infinitely flowing and *flowering* in form.

✳ We are each a witness and *creator* of our own choices.

✳ The *balance* between your creative soul and your self-maintaining body allows you to experience the present moment.

✳ Your soul *loves* you.

✳ Your soul is *always* steady and stable.

✳ Your soul's truth is your *ultimate* stability.

✳ Surrender yourself to the *wisdom* of your soul.

✳ Resisting the flow of life is *futile.*

✳ Relaxation is *key.*

✳ Relax and learn while loving *each moment.*

Now is Attractive

UNDERSTANDING

As a conscious living being, you are inherently *active*. Even when you choose to be *passive*, you are making a choice in how you act. As William Shakespeare so eloquently wrote over 400 years ago for his comedy, "As You Like It":

All the world's a stage,

And all the men and women merely players;

They have their exits and their entrances,

And one man in his time plays many parts

Indeed, we are *all* players acting upon the global stage, because we are all acting through the choices we make. Our world is a *stage*, rather than a movie, and we are the *actors*, not merely the audience.

Regardless of how much you can or cannot see, hear, or otherwise feel the world around you, you are *never* truly isolated. The rest of the world is always on stage *with* you, in this moment and in every moment. This is why you are always subject to external influences.

As you learned in Week 9, we are all living together in *energetic fields* of resonance and opposition. These fields flow and shift, stabilize and destabilize, creating the unending flowering of forms that is life's flow.

In the process of witnessing the effects of these fields, you experience forces of attraction and repulsion in *each moment*. While gravity attracts your body towards the center of the Earth, gravity *also* repels your body from flying off the Earth. This is because repulsion is simply attraction in the opposite direction. In other words, the same way that you are attracted *towards* something, you are also attracted *away* from something else.

The *desires* that you feel are one form of attraction and the desire you feel to support *wellness* is the attraction of love. Attraction is what *empowers* the feminine flow of life. And, it's the feminine flow of life that we observe whenever we witness flows of energy.

THE FLOWING OF ENERGY *INFUSES* ALL LIFE THROUGHOUT OUR UNIVERSE.

As masculinity provides the stability, structure, and guidance to channel the feminine flow of life, it is essential for your masculinity to *guide* the flow of life in support of wellness in each moment rather than to *suppress* the flow. This means that the forces of attraction you experience are to be *directed* in support of wellness while being *felt*, rather than subdued. Since wellness is the *increased* ability to function, to suppress the flow of life is to directly undermine life's wellness.

In each moment, your creative soul is attracting you towards growth while your self-maintaining body is attracting you towards the familiar. This means that how you *act* in response to forces of attraction is always up to you. This is why you are a *player* on the global stage rather than a stage prop. However, to play your part well you must play your part in *wellness*. If you instead stick to acting out past roles, you are choosing to act in fear rather than choosing to act knowingly in love.

When acting on the global stage, not only is your ego your *mask*; it also serves as a *bridge* between your body and your soul. Your *lower self* is your ego's integration with your body. Your *higher self* is your ego's integration with your soul. Your lower self is your identity *in fear*. Your higher self is your identity *in love*.

YOUR EGO EXISTS TO BE *IN SERVICE*, NOT TO BE IN CHARGE.

This is why loosening your body's grip on how you act allows your soul to more freely direct your actions with *love*. In full maturity, your body and ego let go of *all* attempts to control your actions and instead allow your soul to freely *be you*. This process of release allows your body to then be in service to love by following your soul's direction. When your body lives in trust with your soul, you create a *divine union* of love between them that allows for your soul's essence to radiate out into the world *through* your body.

The forms of attraction that you feel as survival, material, and emotional desires are your body's best attempts at managing your life. Yet, your body exists primarily to ensure your *survival,* rather than to manage the complexities of your *thriving.* The more consciously you embody your soul's knowing, the less need you have to rely on your body's instincts.

By witnessing the qualities of your higher self, you are able to reform your ego to *represent* your higher self to others by acknowledging its qualities as yours. This then allows you to identify yourself as your highest and most powerful expression while acting knowingly with love on the world stage.

To knowingly act in each moment, simply:

- *Relax* into your knowing,

- *Feel* into your knowing,

- *Trust* your knowing, and

- *Follow* your knowing.

Though your soul is always attracting you with love, you always have the option of being swayed by *other* forms of attraction. For example, your body is attracted to safety, sex, security, and power. However, your soul *knows* that these things do not need to be sought out.

As an actor on the global stage, you can *trust* that your soul knows the script to the great play of love. Meanwhile, your self-maintaining body *desires* to keep playing past roles in order to feel more secure. So, by choosing to be *present* in each moment, you are able to consciously follow your soul's direction to play your part in love regardless of any resistance you may feel in your body.

FOLLOWING YOUR SOUL'S DIRECTION IS *ESSENTIAL* FOR YOU TO USE THE INTERNAL GUIDANCE SYSTEM YOU'VE BEEN BUILDING THROUGHOUT THIS PROGRAM.

This is because the direction offered by your soul is your soul's knowing, your soul's calling, your soul's truth, and your soul's love. Simply stated, your soul *knows* how to create wellness by acting with love in each moment.

In every moment that you choose to live as an *embodiment* of love, you choose for your soul to direct you towards wellness through your *desire* to love. You are then choosing to play your part, in love, on life's stage. By following the attraction of your soul, you are choosing a life of growth, expansiveness, inspiration, and an *intimate* loving relationship with reality. This is why you will *always* create internal stability and wellness when you "Feel. Love. Now..."

PRACTICE

Goal

The goal for this week is to relax, flex your pelvic muscles, and be present with attraction.

Breath

For this week's portion of your breathing exercise, continue to breathe love as you did in last week's portion.

Movement

For Step 16 of your daily practice, stay on your back, straighten your legs, and place the backs of your heels on the corners of your mat. Place your arms by your sides with your palms facing upwards and relax your body. Extend the back of your head away from your shoulders, with your chin tilted down towards your throat to relieve any tension in your neck. If your body feels cool, you're welcome to have a blanket on top of you.

On your inhalation, repeatedly squeeze your pelvic muscles on the front side of your body. If you're not familiar with your frontal pelvic muscles, they're the muscles you use to stop the flow in the middle of peeing.

With practice, it's possible to discern your pelvic muscle groupings with roughly 5 in the front and 5 in the back. So, if you are familiar with your frontal pelvic muscles, you can squeeze them individually from the top down repeatedly as you inhale.

On your exhalation, repeatedly squeeze your pelvic muscles on the back side of your body. If you're not familiar with your posterior pelvic muscles, they're the muscles you use to stop in the middle of defecating. If you *are* familiar with your posterior pelvic muscles, you can squeeze them individually from the bottom up repeatedly as you exhale.

As you continue your breathing exercise, repeatedly squeeze your frontal pelvic muscles on each inhalation and your posterior pelvic muscles on each exhalation for a count of 10 breaths. As always, your breathing exercise is the most important part of your practice. So, focus on keeping your breathing slow, deep, and even as you remain present with attraction.

Steps

	FOCUS	MOVEMENT	BREATH
1	Feel your sensations	Standing straight	Stage 1
2	Feel your emotions	Forward Folding	Stage 2
3	Feel your cycles	L Position	Stage 3
4	Feel your self	Arms behind & fold	Stage 4
5	Feel your relationships	Downward dog & splits	Stage 5
6	Feel your world	Head rolling	Stage 6
7	Love life	Torso extending	Loving
8	Love yourself	Hip revolving	Loving
9	Love the contrasts	Torso rotating	Loving
10	Love beauty	T twisting	Loving
11	Love one another	Vinyasa	Loving
12	Love each moment	Push-ups	Loving
13	Be present with the past	Cat-cow & lean back	Loving
14	Be present with creation	Squatting	Loving
15	Be present with life's flow	Sit-ups	Loving
16	Be present with attraction	PM-flexing	Loving

Beyond

Outside of your practice, *be present with attraction* by observing the desires you feel, regardless of any judgments you may have about those desires. In the process, you'll discover that you are always free to choose how you play your part on life's stage. If you ever have any difficulty, simply practice your breathing exercise and "Feel. Love. Now..." As always, be sure to do your practice *every day*, for 7 days, before starting Week 17.

QUESTIONS

Every day, after you do the practice portion of this week's lesson, ask yourself these questions and discover what answers are true for you in the moment.

- ➕ What are you feeling attracted to in this moment?

- ➕ Do you feel the difference between your desire to love versus your other desires?

- ➕ Are you accepting of what you are attracted towards?

- ➕ Are you accepting of what you are attracted away from?

- ➕ Do you feel the balance of attraction between your body and soul?

- ➕ Do you feel both your masculinity and your femininity?

- ➕ Are you resisting doing your daily practice?

- ➕ Are you relaxing into any discomfort?

- ➕ Are you feeling more stable and at peace than you were before today's practice?

- ➕ Are you feeling freer than you were before today's practice and, if not, what's in the way of you feeling freer?

- ➕ Are you waking up to the truth of each moment?

- ➕ How does the flowering of life feel to you?

- ➕ Are you present with attraction?

REVIEW

After answering the list of questions on the *seventh day*, see how much you've mastered this week's lesson by observing whether you've come to realize or understand these key insights:

* ✳ You are inherently *active*, even when choosing to be passive.

* ✳ The world is a *stage*, rather than a movie.

* ✳ We are *actors* on the world stage, not merely the audience.

* ✳ You act on the world stage through the *choices* you make.

* ✳ To play your part *well* you must play your part in *wellness*.

* ✳ When it's time for something to be *actual*, that's when you act.

* ✳ Acting from irritation is to prioritize *ideas* over reality.

* ✳ You are *never* truly isolated.

* ✳ You experience forces of attraction and repulsion in *each* moment.

* ✳ Repulsion is simply attraction in the *opposite* direction.

* ✳ Attraction *empowers* the feminine flow of life.

* ✳ The flow of life is a flow of *energy* that infuses all life throughout our Universe.

* ✳ You can make choices that *energize* you or choices that *drain* you.

✳ Choose for your masculinity to *guide* the flow of life, rather than to suppress it.

✳ To support wellness, the attraction you feel must be *felt* while being directed.

✳ Your creative soul attracts you towards *growth*.

✳ Your self-maintaining body attracts you towards the *familiar*.

✳ How you *respond* to forces of attraction in each moment is always your choice.

✳ Your *ego* serves as both a mask and a bridge between your body and your soul.

✳ Your lower self is your ego's integration with your *body*.

✳ Your higher self is your ego's integration with your *soul*.

✳ Your lower self is your identity in *fear*.

✳ Your higher self is your identity in *love*.

✳ Your ego exists to be in *service*, not to be in charge.

✳ Loosening your body's grip on how you *act* allows your soul to more freely direct your actions.

✳ Your soul is able to come forth *through* your being into your doing, when you allow it.

✳ Emotional contraction *disempowers* your soul in response to your body's fears.

✳ In full maturity, your body and ego *let go* of all attempts to control your actions.

✳ You allow your body to be in service to love by *following* your soul's direction.

✳ When your body lives in *trust* with your soul, you create a divine union of love between them.

✳ The *divine union* of body and soul allows for your soul's essence to radiate out through your body.

✳ Your body exists to ensure your *survival* rather than to manage the complexities of *thriving*.

✳ The more *conscious* you are, the less need you have to rely on your body's instincts.

✳ Expanding your capacity to be present with attraction requires *discipline*.

✳ Truly *understanding* the present requires discipline.

✳ Your higher self is your highest source of *confidence*.

✳ By making choices, you navigate among *different*, ever-changing realities.

✳ To act *knowingly*, relax into, feel into, trust, and follow your knowing.

✳ Your soul *knows* the script to the great play of love.

✳ Your body desires to keep playing *past* roles.

✳ To *re-enact* your past roles is to act in fear rather than to act in love.

✳ It's easy for you to direct your body but *impossible* for you to direct your soul.

✳ Your body only learns through *experience*.

✳ Your inner conflicts *resolve* themselves through experience.

✳ By choosing to be truly *present*, you are able to follow your soul's direction.

✳ To follow your soul's direction is to choose an *intimate* relationship with reality.

✳ Being present creates intimacy with the *world*.

✳ Fear *impedes* intimacy.

✳ Your relationship with others *reflects* your relationship with the world.

✳ To follow the direction of your soul is to agree to what you're *not yet* ready for but soon will be.

✳ Feel the *truth* of how safe you are in each moment.

✳ With love, there's fundamentally *nothing* to worry about.

✳ Resisting the attraction you feel towards love is *futile*.

✳ Relaxation is *key*.

✳ Relax and learn while loving *each moment*.

Now is Beautiful

UNDERSTANDING

Because you have free will, you are *free* to live a beautiful life. The direction that your soul provides you with is not a *substitute* for your freedom; it's complementary to it. As an actor in the great play of life, how you choose to play your roles is up to you, no matter how closely you follow or ignore your lines.

Even though your soul provides you with loving direction and guidance in each moment, your soul attaches no expectation nor punishment to your choices. Certainly, illness itself does an adequate job of being its own punishment!

FEEL. LOVE. NOW... SUPPORTS NOT ONLY YOUR PHYSICAL, MENTAL, AND EMOTIONAL WELLNESS BUT ALSO YOUR *SPIRITUAL* WELLNESS.

Your spiritual wellness is your increased ability to be in *alignment* with the truth of love, as directed by your soul. Essentially, your spirit is your body's *access* to your soul. The wellness of your spirit is what allows you to maintain a high *frequency* while also maintaining a high *intensity* in your spiritual vibrations.

Seeing as spiritual vibrations are the vibrations of consciousness itself, you may be wondering how it is that consciousness is able to vibrate in the first place. In other words, what is it that *allows* consciousness to vibrate?

Well, it turns out that consciousness vibrates because it is subject to the ultimate force of *attraction*. In the same way that a guitar string needs tension in order to vibrate, the ocean of consciousness *also* needs tension in order to vibrate. This tension is the universal force of attraction towards equilibrium, known as Divine Love. This ultimate force is known as Divine Love because it is the source of *all* love, *all* attraction, and *all* beauty.

Divine Love is what *holds* our Universe together in equilibrium as a single living being. It's how your soul *knows* the way to direct you with love. It's also the *basis* of every technology and scientific discovery.

Divine Love is what *allows* for the flowering of form and the flow of life. It's what *allows* for the creation of each present moment. It's what *allows* consciousness to be expressed as reality.

Divine Love is what allows for illness while simultaneously attracting life towards wellness. It's what allows the forms of life to be *finite* while allowing the flow of life to be *infinite*. This means that both wellness and illness are *infinite* and cannot be quantified. Instead, wellness and illness can only be measured as relative *fractions* of infinity.

As the ocean of consciousness is an infinite ocean of possibility, the flow of life is an infinite flow of information, powered by Divine Love. Because information is *communicable*, illness and wellness are *also* communicable.

As human beings, we are only able to comprehend *correlated* patterns in the flow of information. Yet, patterns of correlation *do not* determine causation. Instead, correlations suggest *potential* causes and effects, making it easy for us to *misidentify* the effects of an illness as being its causes. In confusing cause with effect, it becomes easy to mistakenly punish the ill for their illness. In reality, causation is determined by the *functioning* of our Universe, made *real* by Divine Love.

ARE YOU REALIZING NOW JUST HOW *BEAUTIFUL* REALITY IS?

When you realize something, what you are doing is revealing truth beyond your prior limitations. You are revealing the *beauty* of the truth of reality. Because your eyes only see the narrow bandwidth of light that you can visually process, most of reality is *unseen* and indeed *cannot* be seen with your eyes. This is why the beauty of reality is revealed not just by your bodily senses but also by your mind, heart, and spirit.

As beauty is the combination of an entity's aspects that you feel as pleasurable – and pleasure is only felt in each moment, beauty only exists in the now. This is why now is *beautiful*.

Each present moment is a beautiful gift of Divine Love, allowing us to act freely and lovingly in the great play of life. Your soul is *beautiful* and is always present to direct you with love in harmony with the Universe, the Source of all creation. By choosing to live as an embodiment of your soul's truth, you create wellness in your life as a shining light of love for *all*.

PRACTICE

Goal

The goal for this week is to relax, be at peace, and be present with beauty.

Breath

For this week's portion of your breathing exercise, let go of *any* effort in your breathing. Instead, close your mouth to breathe through your nose if you can. Let your body breathe naturally and effortlessly without any need to think. Let go of your thoughts. Let go of every layer of your breathing exercise that you've practiced up until this step. It's time to rest.

Movement

For Step 17 of your daily practice, remain on your back, close your eyes, and just rest. Feel whatever is present for you, without judging any of it. Instead, simply observe the beauty of being alive.

Witness the beauty of being at peace, no matter what is present for you on the inside or the outside. There is nothing to strive for now, no need to count breaths.

There's no need to rush ahead or concern yourself with things to be done. Instead, allow your soul to determine the duration of your rest. It will direct you when to get up.

Steps

	FOCUS	MOVEMENT	BREATH
1	Feel your sensations	Standing straight	Stage 1
2	Feel your emotions	Forward Folding	Stage 2
3	Feel your cycles	L Position	Stage 3
4	Feel your self	Arms behind & fold	Stage 4
5	Feel your relationships	Downward dog & splits	Stage 5
6	Feel your world	Head rolling	Stage 6
7	Love life	Torso extending	Loving
8	Love yourself	Hip revolving	Loving
9	Love the contrasts	Torso rotating	Loving
10	Love beauty	T twisting	Loving
11	Love one another	Vinyasa	Loving
12	Love each moment	Push-ups	Loving
13	Be present with the past	Cat-cow & lean back	Loving
14	Be present with creation	Squatting	Loving
15	Be present with life's flow	Sit-ups	Loving
16	Be present with attraction	PM-flexing	Loving
17	Be present with beauty	Resting	Natural

Beyond

Outside of your practice, *be present with beauty* by observing the marvelousness of reality. If you ever have any difficulty, simply practice your full breathing exercise and "Feel. Love. Now…"

Be sure to do your practice *every day*, for 7 days, before starting Week 18. You're almost there!

QUESTIONS

Every day, after you do the practice portion of this week's lesson, ask yourself these questions and discover what answers are true for you in the moment.

- Do you feel the beauty of this moment?

- Do you feel how Divine Love is holding the Universe together?

- Are you aware of how truly free you are?

- How fully are you observing what Divine Love is allowing you to experience?

- How does the flow of life feel to you in this moment?

- Are you relaxed in the beauty of being you?

- Are you allowing life to flow with love?

- Are you feeling more stable and at peace than you were before today's practice?

- Are you feeling freer than you were before today's practice and, if not, what's in the way of you feeling freer?

- Are you waking up to the beauty of each moment?

- Are you waking up to the beauty of loving life?

- Are you present with beauty?

REVIEW

After answering the list of questions on the *seventh day*, see how much you've mastered this week's lesson by observing whether you've come to realize or understand these key insights:

* You are *free* to live a beautiful life.

* How you choose to *play* your roles is up to you.

* Your soul attaches no expectation *nor* punishment to your choices.

* Your spirit is your body's *access* to your soul.

* Your spirit is your *intuitive* connection.

* Spiritual wellness is the increased ability to be in *alignment* with the truth of love.

* Spiritual wellness allows you a high *frequency* and a high *intensity* of spiritual vibration.

* You can feel the spiritual vibrations of others *without* resonating with them.

* Consciousness vibrates because it is subject to the force of *Divine Love*.

* Divine Love is the universal force of *attraction* towards equilibrium.

* Divine Love is the source of *all* attraction, *all* beauty, and *all* love.

✳ Divine Love *holds* the Universe together in equilibrium as a single living being.

✳ Divine Live is how your soul *knows* the way to direct you with love.

✳ Divine Love is the *basis* of every technology and scientific discovery.

✳ Divine Love *allows* for the flowering of form and the flow of life.

✳ Divine Love allows for the *creation* of each present moment.

✳ Divine Love allows consciousness to be *expressed* as reality.

✳ Divine Love allows for illness while *attracting* life towards wellness.

✳ Divine Love allows the forms of life to be *finite* and the flow of life to be *infinite*.

✳ Wellness and illness are infinite and *cannot* be quantified.

✳ Wellness and illness can only be measured as relative *fractions* of infinity.

✳ The flow of life is an infinite flow of *information*, powered by Divine Love.

✳ Divine Love *rules* the Universe.

✳ We only comprehend *correlated* patterns in the flow of information.

✳ Patterns of correlation *don't* determine causation.

✳ Causation is determined by how reality *functions*.

✳ The *effects* of illness are easily misidentified as being its causes.

✳ Punishing the ill for their illness *confuses* cause with effect.

✳ Illness and wellness are *communicable* because information is communicable.

✳ When you *realize* something, you are revealing truth beyond prior limitations.

✳ Most of reality is *unseen* and cannot be seen with your eyes.

✳ Expanding your capacity to be present with beauty requires *discipline.*

✳ Truly *understanding* the present requires discipline.

✳ Being present is how you follow the ideal *path* of your becoming.

✳ Now is *beautiful.*

✳ Beauty *only* exists in the now.

✳ Your soul is always present to direct you in *harmony* with love.

✳ You create *wellness* by choosing to live as an expression of your soul's truth.

✳ Each present moment is a beautiful *gift* of Divine Love.

✳ Resisting the beauty of Divine Love is *futile.*

✳ Relaxation is *key.*

✳ Relax and learn while loving *each moment.*

Now is What Is

UNDERSTANDING

Your life is not an accident, because God doesn't make mistakes. Your life is on purpose, because *life* is on purpose.

The life you experience in each moment is entirely *intentional*. It's the result of a collective decision, by the single living being we are, to create reality in each moment from the choices we make and to witness our shared existence as individuals.

> ## LIFE IS THE *TRUTH OF CONSCIOUSNESS* REVEALING ITSELF TO ITSELF.

The intention of our collective experience of reality is to progress from ignorance into knowledge and from the folly of obliviousness into the wisdom of caring. Knowing leads to *being*, which leads to *doing*, which leads to *having*, all of which lead to *more* knowing. This is why your destiny is not a destination – but rather a journey.

Though your body was conceived and grows, diminishes and will eventually die, as an aspect of consciousness itself you are *infinite* and always safe. From this current reality into realities past or yet to be formed, your soul is always guiding you with love. It is not your job to plan out the manifestations of your soul, of other souls, nor of the collective of souls. Everything has its place, *regardless* of your understanding of it.

Understanding reality facilitates peace and stability in the midst of illusion. It is by *embodying* peace that you are able to be fully present in each moment. Regardless of external factors, you receive your soul's guidance most fully when you are at peace within yourself. This is why relaxing into inner peace results in inner stability.

As your body learns the truth of its reality, peace within yourself is *inevitable*. So, recognize truth in each moment instead of seeking to answer how can it be. In realizing who you truly are, you experience *spiritual bliss*.

Spirituality is not a *part* of your life but rather the *core* of it. This is because spirituality is the process of aligning your body with your soul's truth by learning more about reality as it *truly* is. It's why spirituality cannot be developed separately from any other aspect of your life and is ultimately essential for your wellness and stability.

Grounded spirituality takes place *in* reality. This grounding within reality is what differentiates spirituality from psychosis. Illusions provide a *contextual* field for you to experience. They offer a way to know the darkness of ignorance, a way to know what is *not*. Illusions are the darkness that allows the reality of what is to be *revealed* by the light of Divine Love.

God *is* the Universe and the Source of all creation in its omniscient totality. You can *know* God but you cannot *think* God. God gives *direction*, not correction; *commendation*, not condemnation. The denial of Divine Love as God's love is the only way to be truly lost in the illusions of your existence. Embracing Divine Love with peace is what enables you to *complete* your internal guidance system, to be guided towards a life of stability and wellness in each moment.

You receive God's love in the ways that you love God. As God loves life, it is only through the *uninhibited* loving of life in each moment that you are able to experience holiness: Feel. Love. Now... is what is.

Assertions of *truthfulness*, statements of what is, reinforce your awareness in alignment with truth. They form the basis of holy prayer, which is a spiritual technology used to reorient your awareness towards the truth of Divine Love.

Mantras, yantras, mandalas, meditations, and other spiritual technologies are *also* available to support you in aligning your awareness. Yet, like all technologies, spiritual technologies have power and can be misused to reorient your awareness *away* from truth. Like fire, power is both useful and dangerous. So, relax into what is. Listen, trust, and follow the guidance of your soul's knowing in each moment. Be at peace and rest in your knowing of Divine Love.

Your soul grants you access to information in the *moment* you are ready to receive it. In each moment, you are invited to embrace the light of the wisdom of true knowing from within the darkness of the illusion of ignorance.

Your intellect is a blessing, as it allows you to more effectively discern and learn while on your path of enlightenment, which is your path to true knowledge. Yet, thought is never a *replacement* for knowledge; knowing must be *experienced*.

So, love life in each moment. Even as you create stability and wellness in your life and for *all* life, accept what is *as* it is. Be at peace with your life and with all life. Now *is* what is. As you proceed along the magnificent journey that *is* life itself, know that you are ultimately safe – and that *all* will be revealed by the light of Divine Love as you *progress* through the life you are living and all subsequent lifetimes.

PRACTICE

Goal

The goal for this week is to relax, meditate, and be present with what is.

Breath

For this week's portion of your breathing exercise, continue to let go of any effort or intervention with your breathing. In each moment, allow your body to breathe what is.

Movement

For this final step of your daily practice, come to sit in meditation. While there are many *ways* to sit in meditation, be sure to sit comfortably while sitting up straight. Similar to *standing* up straight, it may help you to imagine a string tugging the crown of your head *upward* with another string tugging your tailbone *downward*.

Whether using cushions, bolsters, stools, or whatever else may be available for you to sit on, have your knees and butt act as 3 stable points of contact with whatever stable surfaces are available. These 3 points should form a stable and even, isosceles triangle.

To prevent strain on your body, have your knees be at a lower elevation than your hips. The less flexible your hips are, the greater the elevation difference you will need in order to remain comfortable.

Once you've come to sit up straight and comfortably, close your eyes and make the following assertions, with one line per breath, either silently or aloud:

I know who I am, through the grace of Divine Love.

I know what I am, through the grace of Divine Love.

I know how I serve, through the grace of Divine Love.

Now, I am here, in love.

Now, I am known, in love.

Now, I am love, loving love.

Indeed, these assertions are *true* for your higher self. Your higher self *does* know who you are, what you are, and how you serve through the grace of Divine Love, even when your lower self doesn't. In each moment, it is true that you are here, that you are known, and that you are love, loving love, in love. So, once you assert and rest in your knowing, invite your soul and oversoul to ground into the present moment through your body, by stating the following:

I invite the truest essence of my soul.

I invite my oversoul to reveal what is.

Then, simply sit and be present with what is. Without any effort or intervention, feel whatever feelings are present for you. Observe whatever thoughts or visions arise and let them come and go without attachment. Allow yourself to release any judgments and be at peace with the moment you're in.

Without expectations, simply observe what arises within you. Observe whatever it is that your soul and oversoul choose to reveal to you. If you feel contracted or if you don't seem to be feeling much of anything, expand your feelings outwards into the world around you.

If you wish, you may direct your closed eyes to the midpoint between the upper edges of your eyebrows. But, there is no need to look for anything. You've already found it.

Sit in meditation for as long as your soul determines. It will direct you when to get up. And, if you feel the flow of energy coursing through you – calling on you to move or express yourself, let yourself be carried by the flow. Move, express, and dance the dance of life in whatever ways your soul directs. You are now stable and well enough in yourself to listen to the whispers of your intuition and trust in your soul's guidance.

Construction of your real-time navigation system, directing you towards stability and wellness in each moment, is now complete.

FEEL. LOVE. NOW...

Steps

	FOCUS	MOVEMENT	BREATH
1	Feel your sensations	Standing straight	Stage 1
2	Feel your emotions	Forward Folding	Stage 2
3	Feel your cycles	L Position	Stage 3
4	Feel your self	Arms behind & fold	Stage 4
5	Feel your relationships	Downward dog & splits	Stage 5
6	Feel your world	Head rolling	Stage 6
7	Love life	Torso extending	Loving
8	Love yourself	Hip revolving	Loving
9	Love the contrasts	Torso rotating	Loving
10	Love beauty	T twisting	Loving
11	Love one another	Vinyasa	Loving
12	Love each moment	Push-ups	Loving
13	Be present with the past	Cat-cow & lean back	Loving
14	Be present with creation	Squatting	Loving
15	Be present with life's flow	Sit-ups	Loving
16	Be present with attraction	PM-flexing	Loving
17	Be present with beauty	Resting	Natural
18	Be present with what is	Meditating	Natural

Beyond

Outside of your daily practice, *be present with what is* by being at peace with reality. If you ever have any difficulty, simply practice your breathing exercise and "Feel. Love. Now..." Be sure to do your daily practice *every day*, for 7 days, before reading the Section III Review. Although you've completed the *construction* of your internal navigation system, there's more for you to learn about how to *use* it.

QUESTIONS

Every day, after you do the practice portion of this week's lesson, ask yourself these questions and discover what answers are true for you in the moment.

- Do you feel at peace in this moment?

- Do you know your life's purpose?

- Which possibilities are you choosing to make actual, right now?

- Do you trust your soul's guidance?

- Do you feel your ultimate stability?

- Are you embracing your spirituality?

- What is in the way of you loving life more fully?

- Are you feeling more stable and at peace than you were before today's practice?

- Are you feeling freer than you were before today's practice and, if not, what's in the way of you feeling freer?

- Are you grateful for your illusions?

- Are you waking up to the glory of what is?

- Are you present with what is?

REVIEW

After answering the list of questions on the *seventh day*, see how much you've mastered this week's lesson by observing whether you've come to realize or understand these key insights:

* ✳ Your life is *not* an accident, because God doesn't make mistakes.

* ✳ Your life is on purpose, because *life* is on purpose.

* ✳ Your life's purpose exists in *each* moment.

* ✳ Your life is the result of a collective decision to experience possibility through *individuality*.

* ✳ Life is the *truth of consciousness* revealing itself to itself.

* ✳ Life's intention is to *progress* from ignorance into knowledge and obliviousness into caring.

* ✳ Knowing leads to being, leads to doing, leads to having, all of which lead to *more* knowing.

* ✳ Life is an *infinite* fractal loop.

* ✳ Your destiny is a journey, *not* a destination.

* ✳ Your *wellness* is a journey, not a destination.

* ✳ As an aspect of consciousness, you are infinite and *always* safe.

* ✳ Your soul is *always* guiding you with love, even when it guides you to wait.

✳ It is *not* your job to plan out the manifestations of consciousness.

✳ Everything has its place, *regardless* of your understanding of it.

✳ Understanding reality facilitates peace and stability in the *midst* of illusion.

✳ You are able to be fully present in each moment by *embodying* peace.

✳ Your soul's guidance is received most *fully* when you're at peace within yourself.

✳ Peace within yourself is *required* to observe that which is steady or constant.

✳ Meditation *allows you* to observe what is steady or constant.

✳ Surrender to what *is* in order to be at peace.

✳ Surrender to life being as it is in *each* moment.

✳ Giving up on life is *not* surrendering to life.

✳ Inner peace results in inner *stability*.

✳ Peace within yourself is *inevitable* as your body learns the truth of your reality.

✳ Recognize truth in each moment instead of seeking to *answer* how can it be.

✳ You experience *spiritual bliss* in realizing who you truly are.

✳ Spirituality is not a part of your life but rather the *core* of it.

✳ Spirituality is the process of learning more about reality as it *truly* is.

✳ Science cannot save humanity from its ignorance – but *spirituality* can.

✳ Spirituality aligns your *body* with your soul's knowing.

✳ Spirituality cannot be developed *separately* from any other aspect of your life.

✳ Grounded spirituality takes place *in* reality.

✳ Grounding *within* reality is what differentiates spirituality from psychosis.

✳ Illusions provide a *contextual* field for you to experience.

✳ Illusions offer a way to experience ignorance, a way to know what is *not.*

✳ *Not* feeling is the greatest illusion.

✳ Illusions allow the reality of *what is* to be revealed by the light of Divine Love.

✳ God *is* the Universe and the Source of all creation in its omniscient totality.

✳ You can *know* God but you cannot *think* God.

✳ God gives *direction*, not correction – *commendation*, not condemnation.

✳ God cannot hide; God can only be *misidentified*.

✳ The denial of Divine Love as God's love is the *only* true oppression.

✳ Without knowing Divine Love, you are *lost* in your illusions.

✳ You receive God's love in the ways that you love *God*.

✳ You can only experience holiness through the *uninhibited* loving of life.

✳ Assertions of *truthfulness* reinforce your awareness in alignment with truth.

✳ Holy prayer directs awareness to *awaken*.

✳ Holy prayer is a spiritual *technology* for reorienting awareness towards truth.

✳ Spiritual technologies have power and can be used to reorient *away* from truth.

✳ Like fire, power is *both* useful and dangerous.

✳ In each moment, *relax*, listen, trust, and follow the guidance of your soul.

✳ Be at *peace* and rest in your knowing of Divine Love.

✳ All will be *revealed* by the light of Divine Love.

✳ Your soul grants access to information in the *moment* you are ready to receive it.

* Expanding your capacity to be present with what is requires *discipline*.

* Truly *understanding* the present requires discipline.

* Know that you are ultimately *safe*.

* Resisting what is is *futile*.

* Relaxation is *key*.

* Relax and learn while loving *each moment*.

Now is All

Congratulations on completing Section III!

IF YOU'VE DONE ALL OF THE LESSONS AND PRACTICES SO FAR, YOU'RE NOW ABLE TO LIVE A LIFE OF WELLNESS AND STABILITY IN EACH MOMENT!

To see how much progress you've made, please use this opportunity to re-read the review sections for Week 13 through Week 18. Then, once you've done so, see whether you've mastered these key points and discover just how much you've learned:

* *Now* is what is real.

* Wellness is the *harmony* of reality.

* Meaning is the *use* of information by reality.

* Reality is *alive.*

FEEL. LOVE. NOW...

✳ You are able to choose because you are *conscious*.

✳ Guidance can be given and received but not *imposed*.

✳ Free will allows you to experience the *illusion* of time.

✳ In reality, the time is always *now*.

✳ Each moment is a *waymarker*, both a beginning and an end.

✳ The future *will be* relevant when it is present, as the past *was* relevant when it was present, because only the *present* is relevant.

✳ We are all aspects of a single living being that is our Universe in its *entirety*.

✳ Our Universe *is* Source, *is* God, *is* Great Spirit.

✳ Our Universe is *both* consciousness and the manifestation of consciousness.

✳ Our Universe provides a *stage* to act within and be witnessed.

✳ Divine Love is the force of *attraction* towards Universal equilibrium.

✳ The force of attraction allows for *interaction*.

✳ Your soul knows the script to the great play of life *through* Divine Love.

✳ The difference between your soul's knowing and your mind's beliefs is the *mystery of life*.

✳ Facilitating wellness by structuring sequences of choices is what souls *do.*

✳ Your body's conflicts with change are part of the process of achieving *direct access* to your soul.

✳ The healthy *marriage* of your body in reception and your soul in direction is the *divine union.*

✳ Trusting in the divine union allows you to freely dance the *dance* of life with love.

✳ Being truly *present* enables you to knowingly act, with your soul as director.

✳ Divine Love is how your soul *knows* the path of love.

✳ Like wellness, life is a journey, *not* a destination.

✳ As an aspect of consciousness, you are infinite and *ultimately* safe.

✳ The darkness of illusion allows reality to be *revealed* by the light of Divine Love.

✳ You receive the love of the Universe in the *ways* that you love the Universe.

✳ Choose to radiate your *essence* into the world, with love.

✳ Know that *all* will ultimately be revealed by the light of Divine Love.

Now is always the time to feel love.

Epilogue

Now that you've successfully constructed your internal guidance system, now is *always* the time to use it!

Whenever you fully feel and fully love while being fully present, you create stability and wellness to the absolute best of your ability. Yet, since life is a journey rather than a destination, the task of creating wellness is never complete.

You need to *maintain* your daily practice in order to maintain the *benefits* of your daily practice. Of course, you're welcome to change it, customize it, and make it your own. Simply feel the effects of whatever changes you make and then choose whether to keep the changes or adjust them accordingly.

Without restarting your daily practice from scratch, you'll likely find it useful to re-read this book from the beginning. In the process, you just might surprise yourself to discover how much of the lessons you missed the first time, the second time, or even the *tenth* time!

Because you are able to resonate unconsciously with others, it's easy for you to recreate external illness *internally*. So, in order to be well and stable within yourself, maintain your stability and wellness *consciously* and support the wellness of others with love. Beware the praising of illness, no matter how esteemed the source of the praise is, and instead meet people where they're at – with love. To assist yourself and others, you can proclaim spiritual *invocations* of your love, such as by stating:

WITH LOVE, I CALL FORTH
WELLNESS, HAPPINESS, AND PROSPERITY,
IN MY LIFE AND FOR *ALL* LIFE.

Being well *within* yourself allows you to bring that wellness to your relationships, to your communities, your society, and your world. As a beacon of wellness, you are able to *inspire* others to shine more brightly themselves. By consciously choosing to be well, you make it easier for others to *resonate* with your wellness.

So, shine brightly! Be in loving service to our Universe by *embodying* your soul's true essence and radiate it out into the world with love. Embrace the glory of being *you* in your fullest, most loving expression – and remember that, though this is the end, it is also *just* the beginning!

About
the Author

Erez Ascher is a philosopher, author, speaker, advisor, and entrepreneur whose love for humanity and dedication to the well-being of both people and planet have led him to focus on addressing life's most pressing issues.

Mr. Ascher's first book, *Actual Understanding*, illuminates how one can understand reality and actualize wellness at all levels of being. His second book, *Feel. Love. Now...*, applies his research on wellness to offer clear guidance and support to individuals in creating stability and wellness in their lives.

Erez is based in California and travels extensively to share his work. He can be contacted at email@ErezAscher.com. Correspondence regarding *Feel. Love. Now...* can be sent to email@FeelLoveNow.online.